Teacher's Handbook

SRA

Reading LABORATORY®

1c

McGraw Hill

SRA

mheducation.com/prek-12

Send all inquiries to:
McGraw-Hill Education
8787 Orion Place
Columbus, OH 43240

ISBN: 978-0-07-702358-4
MHID: 0-07-702358-7

Printed in the United States of America.

3 4 5 6 7 8 QVS 24 23 22 21 20

Table of Contents

Table of Contents

Preface to the 2020 Edition

A Wealth of Good Reading

For more than sixty years, teachers have been aware of the strengths of *SRA Reading Laboratory*—how it provides individualized skills instruction, permits independent work, promotes students' sense of responsibility, and lets each student move at his or her own rate, according to individual ability. However, there is another aspect of *SRA Reading Laboratory* that deserves to be stressed: the great quantity of good reading passages to be found.

The reading selections in *SRA Reading Laboratory* are by no means just sterile skills exercises. They are a balanced collection of fiction and nonfiction short stories and articles that students actually enjoy reading. In addition, they are sources of a great deal of incidental learning as well—about plants, animals, history, science, technology, discovery, fine arts, social institutions, sports, and different cultures.

Students don't just learn to read better by using *SRA Reading Laboratory;* they discover what it means to become readers. They gain pleasure, information, and—if the ultimate goal succeeds—a lifelong love of reading in all kinds of subject areas. They learn to read for a variety of purposes, and they discover what it is to read in a wide range of content areas. Good reading is not just an incidental aspect of *SRA Reading Laboratory* but one of its principal elements and strengths.

Every new edition of *SRA Reading Laboratory* is updated and improved over previous editions. In this 2020 edition, many of the *Power Builder* selections have been replaced with brand-new selections, while other selections have been edited to bring them up to date. The nonfiction reading selections are enhanced by colorful photographs, and the fictional stories incorporate engaging illustrations to promote comprehension and reading enjoyment.

Equitable Educational Resources

The collection of readings exposes students to a balance of fiction and nonfiction genres, such as classic literature, folktales, fantasy, and informational text. In addition, the readings focus on a variety of topics, including science, technology, history, and cultures. The emphasis on student choice and engagement in ***SRA Reading Laboratory*** provides students with essential knowledge and academic vocabulary which is just as important for a literate reader as are developing the skills of decoding, vocabulary, and structural analysis.

Virtually any interesting reading materials can be used to build skills, but materials relating to our tremendous diversity among cultures will help to build a more equitable education for all students. The ***Power Builder*** selections enable students to gain an understanding and appreciation of worldwide settings, lifestyles, problems, and perspectives.

Social and Emotional Learning

In reading the ***Power Builder*** selections, not only will students find plentiful entertainment, but they also will learn about the consequences of greed and the rewards of kindness, generosity, and honesty. They will read true stories about the accomplishments and struggles of all kinds of people throughout history.

As you use ***SRA Reading Laboratory,*** incorporate the following suggestions in your classroom to instill core social and emotional competencies in students.

- Create a continuously nurturing environment for learning but encourage individual student goal setting and progress. Reward positive behavior and help students feel ownership over their own progress.
- Integrate social and emotional skill building by giving students the opportunity for self-reflection on their own reading process.
- Communicate early and often with students and their families. Have students present their progress at parent-teacher conferences. Encourage students to track their progress and to discuss their difficulties and their successes.
- Empower students to become self-directed learners. Talk about growth mindset and make sure students understand how they can work to improve their skills. Encourage students to persist when faced with difficult tasks.

Overview: Getting to Know the Program

Methods and Goals

As a teacher, you know that students differ in how fast they learn as well as in how much they learn. A typical classroom has many levels of learning. Therefore, there is a great need for a systematic way of accommodating all those levels at the same time. ***SRA Reading Laboratory*** does precisely that.

The program meets the differing needs of students by providing multilevel learning materials in one classroom package. It is a complete system offering individualized reading opportunities to all your students. You need no additional materials or teaching assistance to operate it. In fact, it basically operates itself. After some initial training, students manage their own learning. They work independently, score their own work, and keep accurate accounts of their own progress.

The reading materials and associated skills exercises in any one ***Reading Laboratory*** are organized into a series of color-designated difficulty levels that range above and below the average for that grade or age group. The student who reads below grade level finds material that he or she can read right away. This removes the frustration of trying to read and understand material that is too difficult. At the same time, the more advanced student finds materials suited to his or her abilities. This removes the potential boredom that comes with reading materials that are too easy. Students progress according to their own abilities and at whatever pace is appropriate to each one.

You begin using the program in your classroom by working through a series of six Starter Sessions to determine the color level and corresponding Lexile® range in which each student should start. Even if your students have used the program before, it is important to begin each school year with the Starter Sessions and other introductory procedures in order to ensure accurate placement after periods of break time.

Students work individually and chart their progress. Once a week, you may want to have a brief individual conference with each student. By studying the progress charts with the student, you can help the student evaluate his or her work. Then you and the student can decide together whether he or she is ready to move to the next color level.

Goals of SRA Reading Laboratory

1. To develop comprehension, vocabulary, word analysis, and study skills
2. To reinforce specific skills to help students become proficient readers
3. To interest students in reading and to enlarge their specific knowledge, using a wide array of quality fiction and nonfiction selections
4. To develop independent readers with strong comprehension skills, endurance, and confidence
5. To develop the sense of personal responsibility as students take charge of their own learning

Teachers are often surprised to see how much responsibility students can take for their own learning. The more you work with multilevel teaching and learning, the more opportunities you will find for building one-to-one relationships with your students. You will also see how students' self-esteem grows with learning.

The goals of ***SRA Reading Laboratory*** go well beyond mere skills learning, although skills learning is certainly an important part of the whole. Five main goals are served by the various learning materials in ***SRA Reading Laboratory*** and by the educational method and philosophy of the multilevel system.

See Appendix D for a listing of specific comprehension and word-study skills.

If you wish to review in detail the reading skills on which the program is focused, turn to the Comprehension and Word-Study Skills Charts in Appendix D of this handbook. There you can see at a glance the specific skills presented in each reading level and in each ***Power Builder*** within each level.

Getting the Most Out of the Program

A clear understanding of the program will help ensure that you and your students derive maximum benefit from ***SRA Reading Laboratory's*** pedagogical design. Special emphasis is given to these points at the outset so that they will not be overlooked.

1 ***SRA Reading Laboratory*** is a system that has been carefully structured for teaching and developing essential skills and beneficial attitudes in an orderly and purposeful method. When treated as a regularly scheduled part of the classroom routine, the laboratory offers you an organized, systematic program that can significantly improve reading skills, study habits, and feelings of personal responsibility.

2 ***SRA Reading Laboratory*** is a flexible program that can be easily implemented to fit into a variety of school calendars and schedules. One suggestion that has been proven effective is to use the program over a fairly concentrated period of time instead of being widely spaced across the entire school year. The recommended schedule on page 12 calls for eight sessions (twenty to forty minutes long) spaced closely together during the training phase and then followed by a phase in which students use the program materials independently. When practice periods are kept close together, there is carryover learning from one day to the next. When practice periods are spaced too far apart, carryover is lessened, and students tend to forget not only the information learned but even the procedures to follow.

When practice periods are kept close together, there is carryover learning from day to day.

3 It is not intended that every student work his or her way through *all* the ***Power Builders*** in a level or that a student work the ***Power Builders*** in strict sequence. Instead, a student selects (or is given)* ***Power Builders*** in *random* sequence from his or her assigned level; as soon as the student's scores show adequate progress (as discussed on pages 29–32), the student advances to the next color level. Thus, the number of ***Power Builders*** that any student will work in a particular level will vary according to his or her abilities and learning rate. A typical student should probably complete at least four ***Power Builders*** in a level; others may do eight or ten. Some students may require practice with all ***Power Builders*** in a level before moving on.

Students will complete different numbers of ***Power Builders*** depending on their own progress.

4 After the training phase, it is a good idea to begin holding weekly conferences with each student to review his or her progress. You are strongly encouraged to make these conferences mutual consultations in which you and the student decide together whether it is time to move to a new level. Getting students accustomed to taking responsibility for their own learning progress is important if you are to realize the full potential of ***SRA Reading Laboratory*** as not just a builder of skills but of self-image and self-confidence as well.

Encourage students to take responsibility for their own learning.

Although free choice of* ***Power Builders* *by individuals is consistent with the laboratory's purpose and design, the procedure described later in this handbook eliminates individual choice to reduce the confusion resulting from traffic to and from the laboratory box. Student helpers or group leaders can hand out the Progress Charts, Record Pages, and the* ***Power Builders,*** *giving each student any* ***Power Builder*** *that he or she has not yet read in the assigned color level. In this system, the group leaders also collect the materials at the end of the period and refile the* ***Power Builders*** *in the laboratory box. Whether to use this group-leader system or to let each student select his or her materials from the box is up to you.*

Materials

SRA Reading Laboratory contains the following materials:

Teacher's Handbook

The *Teacher's Handbook* contains an overview of *SRA Reading Laboratory* and provides teaching plans for using the program to its maximum advantage. The separate appendixes of the References and Resources section provide detailed information about program selections, skills, and procedures.

The Student Resources section includes a Home Connection letter that should be copied and given to students to take home to provide information to parents and guardians about the program. In addition, the Student Resources section includes the Starter Stories, Record Pages, and Progress Charts. You will copy and distribute these materials as needed.

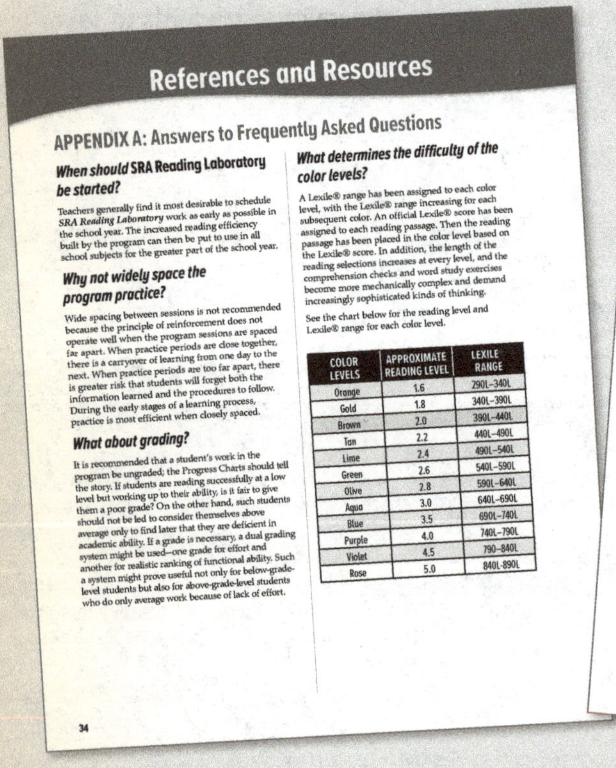

References and Resources

APPENDIX A: Answers to Frequently Asked Questions

When should* SRA Reading Laboratory *be started?

Teachers generally find it most desirable to schedule *SRA Reading Laboratory* work as early as possible in the school year. The increased reading efficiency built by the program can then be put to use in all school subjects for the greater part of the school year.

Why not widely space the program practice?

Wide spacing between sessions is not recommended because the principle of reinforcement does not operate well when the program sessions are spaced far apart. When practice periods are close together, there is a carryover of learning from one day to the next. When practice periods are too far apart, there is greater risk that students will forget both the information learned and the procedures to follow. During the early stages of a learning process, practice is most efficient when closely spaced.

What about grading?

It is recommended that a student's work in the program be ungraded; the Progress Charts should tell the story. If students are reading successfully at a low level but working up to their ability, is it fair to give them a poor grade? On the other hand, such students should not be led to consider themselves above average only to find later that they are deficient in academic ability. If a grade is necessary, a dual grading system might be used—one grade for effort and another for realistic ranking of functional ability. Such a system might prove useful not only for below-grade-level students but also for above-grade-level students who do only average work because of lack of effort.

What determines the difficulty of the color levels?

A Lexile® range has been assigned to each color level, with the Lexile® range increasing for each subsequent color. An official Lexile® score has been assigned to each reading passage. Then the reading passage has been placed in the color level based on the Lexile® score. In addition, the length of the reading selections increases at every level, and the comprehension checks and word study exercises become more mechanically complex and demand increasingly sophisticated kinds of thinking.

See the chart below for the reading level and Lexile® range for each color level.

COLOR LEVELS	APPROXIMATE READING LEVEL	LEXILE RANGE
Orange	1.6	290L–340L
Gold	1.8	340L–390L
Brown	2.0	390L–440L
Tan	2.2	440L–490L
Lime	2.4	490L–540L
Green	2.6	540L–590L
Olive	2.8	590L–640L
Aqua	3.0	640L–690L
Blue	3.5	690L–740L
Purple	4.0	740L–790L
Violet	4.5	790–840L
Rose	5.0	840L-890L

34

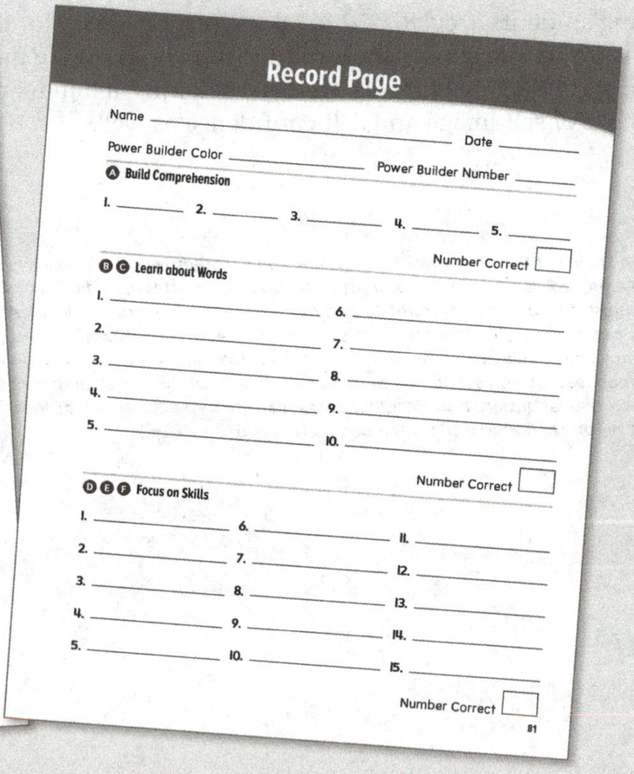

Record Page

Name ____________ Date ______

Power Builder Color ____________ Power Builder Number ______

A Build Comprehension

1. ____ 2. ____ 3. ____ 4. ____ 5. ____

Number Correct ☐

B C Learn about Words

1. ____ 6. ____
2. ____ 7. ____
3. ____ 8. ____
4. ____ 9. ____
5. ____ 10. ____

Number Correct ☐

D E F Focus on Skills

1. ____ 6. ____ 11. ____
2. ____ 7. ____ 12. ____
3. ____ 8. ____ 13. ____
4. ____ 9. ____ 14. ____
5. ____ 10. ____ 15. ____

Number Correct ☐

81

Power Builders

This is the core component of *SRA Reading Laboratory.* The 144 four-page *Power Builders* are arranged in color-coded levels of graduated difficulty. Each *Power Builder* has four parts:

1. High-interest fiction or nonfiction reading selection that includes engaging illustrations or photographs
2. Build Comprehension section that contains multileveled questions about the reading selection
3. Learn about Words section that includes exercises on vocabulary and word-study skills
4. Focus on Skills section that contains a variety of language, reasoning, and comprehension activities

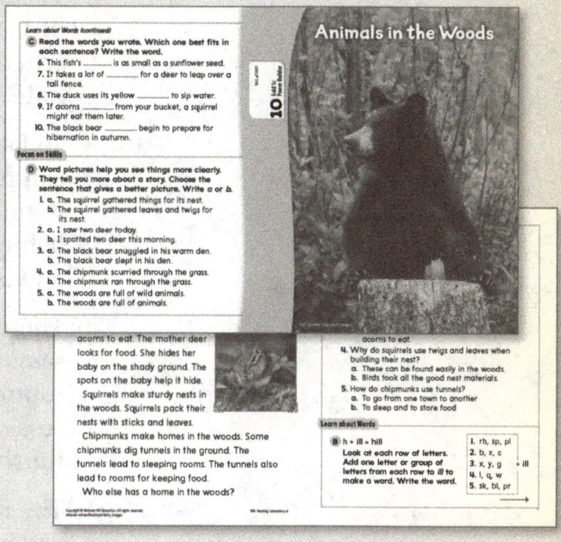

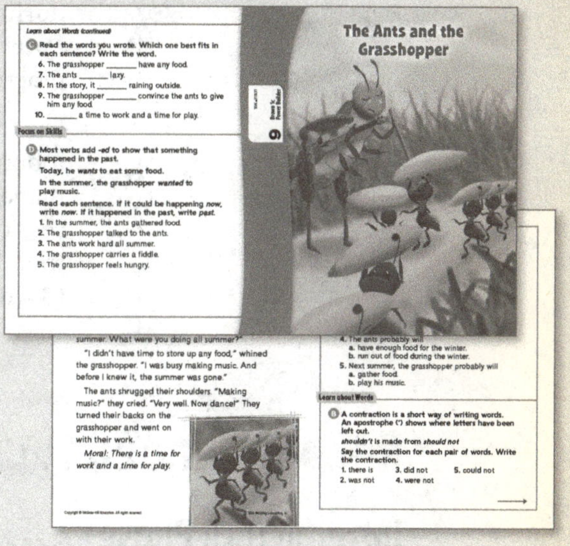

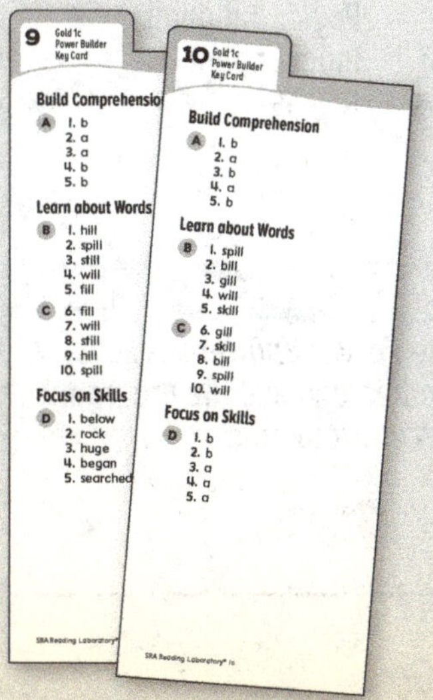

Power Builder Key Cards

Every *Power Builder* has a corresponding *Key Card* with the answers to the *Power Builder* questions. Students use the *Key Card* to score their own work.

Recommended Schedule and Teaching Plans

The following schedule covers a training phase and an independent phase for using the program materials. It is considered best to schedule the *Power Builder* sessions close together. Unless otherwise noted, each session is assumed to be twenty to forty minutes long.

To facilitate instruction, the teaching plans are "scripted" so that you can read them aloud directly to the class if you wish (or paraphrase them if you prefer). These instructions are signaled by shading behind the text. The remaining instruction is for your information and is not meant to be read aloud.

These teaching plans are fully detailed through the first seven sessions. By then the normal laboratory procedures will have become routine, and students will be working independently. The eighth session is also detailed, but it should take place when the class has finished working through the *Power Builders* for the year.

The time of your heaviest involvement in ***SRA Reading Laboratory*** will be the first seven sessions—the introductory training phase during which you will establish students' starting levels, present the ***Power Builder*** component to them, and give them opportunities to practice the basic procedures.

During the remainder of the program, students will be working independently for the most part. Your role will be primarily that of a manager/consultant who sets the times for ***SRA Reading Laboratory*** sessions and holds conferences with individual students to review their progress and help them decide whether they are ready to move to a new level.

Recommended Teaching Schedule

Introductory Phase

SESSION 1	SESSION 2	SESSION 3	SESSION 4	SESSION 5
Student Placement: Starter Stories *Page 13*	Reading Laboratory Introduction *Page 18*	Power Builder Procedures *Page 20*	Power Builders: Independent Use *Page 22*	Power Builders: Comprehension and SQR Formula *Page 25*

SESSION 6	SESSION 7	INDEPENDENT PHASE	SESSION 8
Power Builders: More Comprehension Strategies *Page 27*	Power Builders: Individual Conferences *Page 29*	Follow up with more ***Power Builder*** sessions, spaced closely together, and end the program with a final analysis or evaluation.	Final Evaluation *Page 33*

Student Placement: Starter Stories

SESSION 1

Summary: Today you will begin conducting small-group Starter Sessions using the Starter Stories from the Student Resources section of this Handbook. The six Starter Stories are used to determine the color level at which each student should enter the *Power Builder* component. The Starter Stories also give students a first taste of what it is like to read a ***Power Builder*** story and answer the associated questions. Depending on your class size and schedule, these Starter Sessions may take up to two weeks to complete.

Procedures

Starter Sessions are best conducted with small groups of students (no more than nine at a time) so that you can observe each student's performance and offer help as appropriate.

The most convenient sequence is to take one group through Session 1, providing complete support, then another group, then another, until all students who are ready have been through Session 1. Then you will take each group through Session 2, and so on.

Make copies of the first Starter Story on pages 57–60 and the Record Page on page 81. Distribute the copies to each student.

Read aloud or paraphrase the instructions in the shaded boxes.

THIS is a *Power Builder Starter Story*. By finding out how well each of you reads, we'll decide the best place for each of you to start becoming an even better reader. How do we do this? We work together to read some Starter Stories and answer questions about them. Today we will read Starter 1.

Look at the title and the cover of the story.

Teach Starter 1 as you would teach any group reading lesson. Have the group discuss the pictures. Let them relate individual experiences that come to mind. Put less-familiar words on the board, and have students pronounce them and discuss their meanings. Ask students what they think the story is about and what they may find out when they read it. Then read the story aloud to them, and discuss it briefly to make sure they understand it. Next give them time to read the story silently to themselves.*

NOW you are going to answer some questions about the story we just read. Look at the Record Page. First write your name and today's date at the top of the page. You will always write your answers on a Record Page like this one. Never write on a ***Power Builder*** because other students will use it after you. Now turn back to the story and look at the page with the questions.

Read the directions for Section A, Build Comprehension. Answer any questions students have.

WRITE your answer to each question on the lines on the Record Page. For example, the answer to Question 1 is *a* or *b*. So you will choose the letter you think is correct and write that letter on the first line. What do you think is the answer to Question 1? Yes, it's *a, the way Crow gets all the cake.* Write *a* on the first line next to Number 1. If you don't know an answer as you are working with the Starters or with the ***Power Builders*** on your own, just draw a circle in the blank on your Record Page.

For this Starter, ask and answer every question as a group. When Section A is completed, have students look at Section *B,* Learn about Words. Point out the line next to the letter *B,* and read the segmented word and then the blended word aloud. Read the directions, and answer any questions.

LOOK at the letters next to the number 1. Which of those groups of letters can you add to *ow* to make a word. Yes, *gr* + *ow* make *grow.* Write *grow* in the blank next to 1 in the Learn about Words section on your Record Page.

****By approaching the story in this way, you have led students through a simplified version of the Survey-Question-Read (SQR) method of approaching written material. If at a later time you want to describe the method explicitly so students can consciously practice the technique in their independent work, follow the procedure detailed in Session 5 on pages 25–26.***

Continue with the remaining items, reading each new blended word with the whole group. Then read the directions for Section C, and answer any questions that students may have. Next read aloud the first sentence in this section.

LOOK at the words you wrote in Learn about Words on the Record Page. Which of those words makes sense in the sentence I just read? (*Reread the sentence.*) Yes, the best word is *know; They didn't know where the cake came from.* Write *know* in the blank next to 6 in Section C.

After working through all the items in Section C, read the directions for Section D, Focus on Skills.

EACH of these items will have the word *it* in it. Read along as I read the first item aloud. Then tell me which answer tells what *it* means in that item. (*Read Item 1 aloud.*) Which answer tells what *it* means? Yes, in this sentence *it* means *b, a cake,* so write *b* in the blank next to 1 in Section D on the Record Page.

When you have worked through all the items in Section D and students have written their answers to the exercises, point out that there are some leftover blanks on the Record Page. Tell them not to worry about those. Some levels of the ***Power Builders*** have enough questions to fill every blank on the Record Page.

Copy the Starter Answer Key on page 94 for each student to check his or her responses. Show them how the numbers on the Starter Answer Key correspond to the numbers on their Record Page. Demonstrate the techniques of circling each wrong answer and writing the correct response next to the error.

Record each student's progress on the Reading Progress Chart for Gold. Write *S-1* to represent *Starter 1* in the box for the ***Power Builder*** number. Use a pencil to fill in each correct answer in each section.

My Reading Progress Chart: Gold Level

Fill in the box for each correct answer on your Power Builder.

Power Builder Number	Date	A Build Comprehension	B C Learn about Words	D Focus on Skills
S-1	Oct. 12	1 2 3 4 5	1 2 3 4 5 6 7 8 9 10	1 2 3 4 5
		1 2 3 4 5	1 2 3 4 5 6 7 8 9 10	1 2 3 4 5
		1 2 3 4 5	1 2 3 4 5 6 7 8 9 10	1 2 3 4 5
		1 2 3 4 5	1 2 3 4 5 6 7 8 9 10	1 2 3 4 5

Placement Chart

Each student's starting level should be the highest level at which he or she can successfully read the selection, complete the exercises independently, and follow through accurately on procedures. As each student reaches his or her frustration level, as described below, the student will leave the Starter group and begin working independently one level lower than the Starter Story that is causing problems. General rules for determining frustration level are as follows:

- The student needs to be told as many as one-tenth of the words.
- The student scores lower than eighty percent on the exercises.
- The student relies heavily on the teacher for directions.
- The student takes an inordinate amount of time to finish.

As students continue through the Starter Stories, use the following chart to determine each student's starting level.

Placement Chart for Reading Laboratory 1c

Frustration Level	Beginning Power Builder Level
Starters 1 and 2 (Gold Level)	Orange Level (Lexile® 290L–340L)
Starter 3 (Brown Level)	Gold Level (Lexile® 340L–390L)
Starter 4 (Lime Level)	Tan Level (Lexile® 440L–490L)
Starter 5 (Olive Level)	Green Level (Lexile® 540L–590L)
Starter 6 (Blue Level)	Aqua Level (Lexile® 640L–690L)
All Starters read with ease	Blue Level (Lexile® 690L–740L)

When students work through Starter 2, you should again supervise and provide complete support. Make sure students complete each Starter before checking their answers. As they work through Starter 3, help those who are still unsure of procedures, but allow each student to work as independently as possible. Tell them you want to see how well they remember what to do. Make sure students understand that they should look back at the story if they don't remember the answers. Remind them to put a circle in the blank and go on if they still can't find the answer.

In the coming days, continue through all six Starter Stories, encouraging greater independence with each Starter. As soon as a student's level is established, move the student into the ***Power Builder*** according to the Placement Chart guidelines. Note that Starters 1 and 2 correspond to the Gold level of ***Power Builders***; Starters 3, 4, 5, and 6 correspond to Brown, Lime, Olive, and Blue, respectively.*

As groups of students complete the Starter Stories, move on to Session 2 with them.

***If a student's Lexile® level is already known, you may place the student in the level that corresponds to his or her Lexile® level. If you question the student's Lexile® level, you can use the Starter Stories to confirm the placement level.**

Reading Laboratory Introduction

SESSION 2

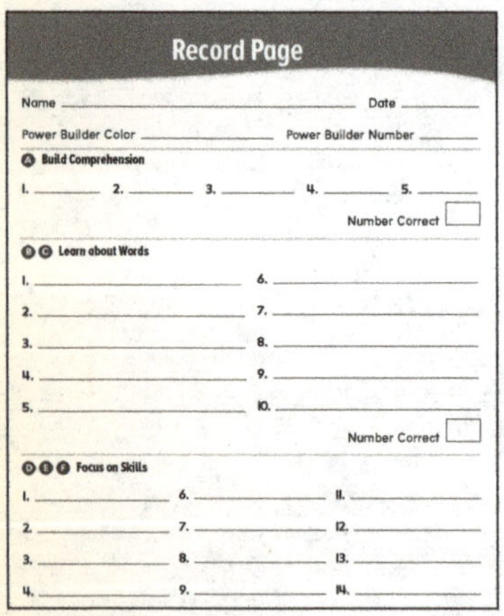
Record Page

Name ______ Date ______

Power Builder Color ______ Power Builder Number ______

A Build Comprehension

1. ___ 2. ___ 3. ___ 4. ___ 5. ___

Number Correct

B C Learn about Words

1.	6.
2.	7.
3.	8.
4.	9.
5.	10.

Number Correct

D E F Focus on Skills

1.	6.	11.
2.	7.	12.
3.	8.	13.
4.	9.	14.

Summary: Today you will introduce *SRA Reading Laboratory* to students and acquaint them with the components of the program.

Procedures

Talk with students about the results of the Starter Stories they completed. Explain that there are various reading levels in the class. Hold up the Orange 4 *Power Builder.*

> **THIS** is a *Power Builder*, and it's just like the Starter Stories. First it has an interesting story. Then it has questions like the ones you answered for the Starter Stories.
>
> The 144 *Power Builders* are grouped according to color. This *Power Builder* is story 4 from the Orange level. [Point to the orange color and the number 4 on the *Power Builder.*] One of these colors will be just right for you as you start out–not too easy and not too hard. When you have material that is just right for you, you can read more easily. I'll tell each of you what color you should start with, based on your work in the Starter Stories. Later you will move to other colors.

Make a copy of the Record Page from page 81 and hold it up.

> **THIS** is a *Power Builder* Record Page. You will write all your answers to the *Power Builder* questions on a Record Page. You must never write on a *Power Builder* because other students will use it after you.

Hold up the Orange 4 ***Power Builder Key Card.***

THIS is a ***Power Builder Key Card.*** When you read the Starter Stories, you used the Starter Answer Key to check your answers. Just as the Starter Answer Key has the answers to the questions for the Starter Story, a ***Power Builder Key Card*** has the answers to the questions for a ***Power Builder.***

[Point to the orange color and the number 4 on the ***Key Card.***] Each ***Power Builder*** has its own ***Key Card.*** This is the ***Key Card*** for the Orange 4 ***Power Builder.*** Look at the orange color. It corresponds to the orange color on the ***Power Builder.*** Now look at the number 4. This is the same number as the ***Power Builder.*** The color and the number of the ***Key Card*** should always match the color and the number of the ***Power Builder.*** This is how you can tell that you are using the correct ***Key Card.***

If you find you've made a mistake, you should always look back at the ***Power Builder*** to see where you have misunderstood. If you have trouble understanding or agreeing with an answer on the ***Key Card,*** feel free to discuss it with me.

Explain that in the next session students will work through a ***Power Builder*** and learn how to keep a record of their work.

SESSION 3

TIP: For organization, have students record their answers in a notebook or have a designated folder for each student to keep track of his or her Record Pages and Progress Charts.

Summary: Today you will work with students individually or in groups of no more than three or four so they can learn the *Power Builder* procedures. If students are working in groups, make sure all students are working in the same color. You will also show students how to check and record their progress.

Procedures

Before the session, choose a *Power Builder* for each student based on his or her assigned color level. Make a copy of the Record Page and the Progress Chart for the appropriate *Power Builder* level for each student. Distribute the chosen *Power Builder* and the copies to each student.

YOU have been reading Starter Stories and answering the questions. You have learned how to record your answers on a Record Page. Today we will work through a *Power Builder* together to see how you will follow a similar procedure with the *Power Builders.* Ordinarily you will each work independently with your *Power Builders,* but today I will lead you through the process.

Have students read their *Power Builders* silently. Then instruct students to write their names and the date in the spaces at the top of the Record Page.

REMEMBER that you will always write your answers on pages like this one. Never write on a *Power Builder.*

The next space is for the *Power Builder* color. There you will write the name of the color level in which you are working. After that there is a space for you to write the number that is on your *Power Builder.*

Make sure students know where to find the color and number of their *Power Builders* and where to fill in this information on the Record Page.

AFTER reading the selection in the *Power Builder,* there are questions similar to the ones you answered in the Starter Stories. Let's look at those questions. They begin with the heading *Build Comprehension.* Now silently read those questions and write the answers to those questions on your Record Sheet. You may refer back to the story if you are unsure of an answer.

Allow students to continue with the other sections of their ***Power Builders.*** Observe students' work to be sure they are writing their answers in the correct places on the Record Page.

When students have finished recording their answers, show them a ***Power Builder Key Card.***

WHEN you finish a ***Power Builder,*** you will find the ***Key Card*** whose color and number match the ***Power Builder*** you read. You will use the ***Key Card*** to check your answers. If you have a different answer from an answer on the ***Key Card,*** you should draw a circle around your answer and write the correct answer next to it.

Remind students that it is okay to get answers wrong. The questions are not for a grade, but for accurate placement to increase learning.

Give students enough time to check their answers and mark any incorrect answers.

NOW find the heading on your Record Page that says *Build Comprehension.* Look at your answers in the blanks below the heading. Find the box that says *Number Correct.* Count the number of your correct answers. Remember, if you have any answers that are circled, they are to be counted as incorrect answers. Write the number of correct answers in the box. Then do the same thing for the Learn about Words and Focus on Skills exercises.

When students have finished scoring their work, have them look at their Progress Chart.

GO to the first line on the Progress Chart, and write in the number of the ***Power Builder*** you just completed. Then write today's date. Finally use your pencil to fill in the number of each answer you got correct in each section of the ***Power Builder.***

Power Builders: Independent Use

SESSION 4

Summary: Today students will begin working with *Power Builders* independently at their own pace. First, however, you may want to review the *Power Builder* procedures with students. Keep in mind that students may not be able to work entirely independently at this stage. You will probably need to be available to answer a number of questions and assist with procedures.

It is important to answer questions and give help promptly at the moment of need. Students can then quickly move ahead on their own. A major advantage of ***SRA Reading Laboratory*** is that it is student directed and it frees the teacher to give prompt help whenever it is needed.

Encourage students to take responsibility and pride in their independent work and progress.

In general allow approximately twenty to forty minutes for each session with the *Power Builders.* Due to individual differences, students will work at different speeds. Early in the program, some students may require more time to complete a *Power Builder.* Later in the program, some students will finish their work early. However, these students should not begin another *Power Builder.* If work is hurried, a student's work may degenerate into a pointless race with time. If students have time remaining, allow them to do an activity that is a change of pace. For example, you could allow them to read library books or other materials for pleasure.

Procedures

Before the session begins, you will need to decide the general procedure for using *Power Builders* in your classroom. You can either have students select their own *Power Builders* individually, or you may want to appoint group leaders in charge of selecting the *Power Builders* and handing them out.*

Next choose a *Power Builder* for each student based on his or her assigned color level. Make a copy of the Record Page and the Progress Chart for the appropriate *Power Builder* level for each student. Distribute the chosen *Power Builder* and the copies to each student.

***You should establish goals that work for your class. Individual student choice encourages personal responsibility. Assigning group leaders and rotating leadership roles fosters a team approach and encourages leadership skills.*

THIS is the color in which you will start your ***Power Builder*** work. This color was chosen based on the work you did with the Starter Stories. Look at the color and the number showing on your ***Power Builder.*** It is on the edge of your ***Power Builder.*** Your ***Power Builder*** must always be the color that is marked on your Progress Chart.

Look at the number of your ***Power Builder.*** Now look on the Progress Chart. Notice the "Power Builder Number" column. Write the number of your ***Power Builder*** in the first block. Then write today's date in the next column. You will do this each time you receive a new ***Power Builder.*** In this way your chart will always show which ***Power Builders*** you have already completed, so you won't repeat the same one twice.

You can read the ***Power Builders*** within your color in any order. For example, you could read Number 12 first and Number 1 last. You will need to work on ***Power Builders*** within the same color until your scores show that you are ready to move to another level. Most of the time, you will need to complete at least four ***Power Builders*** before going on to a new color. We will have conferences together to help us decide when you should move on to a new level. Remember, your work is not a race. Work at the right pace for you to improve your reading skills. This will be different for everyone.

Have students look at the Record Page.

AFTER you have read the ***Power Builder*** selection, you will use a Record Page to write your answers to the questions. Next you will check your answers against the ***Power Builder Key Card*** that has the same color and number as those on your ***Power Builder.***

Consider having a conference with your students after they complete four stories to see if they are ready to move to the next level.

Encourage students to use their Progress Charts during parent-teacher meetings. Students can explain to their parents or guardians what the Progress Chart demonstrates. This will encourage students to take ownership over their own learning.

Hold up a ***Power Builder*** and a matching ***Key Card*** from the ***Reading Laboratory*** box.

> **REMEMBER** each *Power Builder* has its own ***Power Builder Key Card.*** When you finish your ***Power Builder,*** go to the ***Reading Laboratory*** box, and take the matching ***Key Card*** back to your desk. Using your Record Page and the ***Key Card,*** check your answers. On your Record Page, circle any incorrect answers, and write the correct answer next to each incorrect answer. Don't forget to write the number of correct answers in each box next to the words *Number Correct.*

Now ask students to look at their Progress Chart.

> **FINALLY** you will need to fill the boxes on your Progress Chart. This is an important step in tracking your progress in your reading journey. Using a pencil, fill in the box for each correct answer. Now we have reviewed every step for working with the ***Power Builders.*** You are ready to start working with the ***Power Builders*** on your own. Ask me at any time if you are not sure what to do next.

Have students begin their ***Power Builders.***

Power Builders: Comprehension and SQR Formula

SESSION 5

Summary: Today you will conduct a Comprehension Strategy Lesson with small groups of students before they work through a *Power Builder* on their own. This is the first of two lessons designed to introduce comprehension strategies and metacognitive techniques that will help students get the most from their reading.

Procedures

Hold up ***Power Builder*** Orange-3, *Jinx's Tooth.*

WHEN you read a story, you read sentences that belong together. They all help to tell about one main idea. The main idea is what the story is mostly about. Clues about the main idea will help you understand what you read.

Suppose you saw the question *What is the main idea of this story?* What would you look for in the story in order to choose the correct answer?

Hold up the ***Power Builder*** again and point to each element as you discuss the following list.

Here are some things to do:

- Look at the picture on the cover.
- Read the title.
- Read the first sentence.
- Read the last paragraph.

All these items are clues that will help you find the story's main idea. What do you think the story on this *Power Builder* might be about? How would you answer the question *What is the main idea?*

Accept any reasonable answers that students can justify as a description of the main idea. If a response deals with something that seems unreasonable or illogical, ask the student who offered the response to tell which clues he or she used to find that main idea.

I KNOW you probably want to read the story now to find out whether we were correct about the main idea, but we aren't going to read it today. Why do you suppose it's important to know the main idea of a story before you start to read it? If you have an idea of what the story is about and what you might expect to find out from it, you think about what you're reading, and you understand it better. You might not always want to read the last paragraph because sometimes knowing the ending spoils the surprise of the story. However, looking at the title, studying the picture, and reading the first sentence before you start reading the story are good ways to get ready to understand what you'll be reading.

Next write the word *Survey* on the board, using an oversized *S*.

THIS word is *Survey*. It means "to look over." You have just been surveying a story. Did you think of any questions as you were surveying the story?

When some students have responded, write the word *Question* with an oversized *Q* under the word *Survey*. Under the word *Question*, write the word *Read* with an oversized *R*.

IF you remember SQR, it will help you read and study better. First you survey, then you question, and then you are ready to read. Now let's review what we've learned today.

Conduct a brief review of the four strategies for finding the main idea, as well as the SQR formula.

THESE are steps you can use to help you understand anything you read. Try to remember these steps when you read your *Power Builders* and anything else you read on your own.

Allow students to work independently on their ***Power Builders.***

Power Builders: More Comprehension Strategies

SESSION 6

Summary: Today you will conduct the second Comprehension Strategy Lesson with students.

Procedures

Hold up ***Power Builder*** Orange-3 and ask students to look at the title *Jinx's Tooth*. Then point out the story on the inside of the ***Power Builder***. Remind students that recently they looked at the title, studied the picture, read the first sentence, and read the last paragraph of the story to find the main idea. Call on volunteers to recall their predictions about the story's main idea.

> **KNOWING** the main idea will help you understand what you're reading, but you'll understand it even better if you keep asking yourself questions as you read. In this lesson, we are going to read the story and ask ourselves some questions.

Read aloud the first paragraph of *Jinx's Tooth*.

> **ASK** yourself the following questions to check your thoughts on the main idea. *What did I think the story might be about? What do I know now? Was I correct?*

Confirm students' earlier predictions about the story. Then read aloud the second paragraph of the story.

> **NOW** ask yourself the following question: *Do I understand what I just read in this paragraph?* Tell me in your own words what we just read.

Students' responses will probably be worded much like the original paragraph. Accept any answers that show an understanding of events in that paragraph.

Before You Read

Use your eyes to get clues about the main idea:

- Look at the picture.
- Read the title.
- Read the first sentence.
- Read the last paragraph.

As You Read

Ask yourself these questions to make sure you understand:

- Was I correct about what the story is mostly about?
- Do I understand what I just read?
- What did I learn from this story?

IF you didn't understand what you read, it would be a good idea to read that paragraph again.

Read aloud the last two paragraphs of the story.

NOW we have read the whole story. Ask yourself one last question: *What did I learn from this story?*

Allow students to discuss any aspects of the story that interest them.

As you read a story, ask yourselves the questions we just discussed. These questions will help you get the most out of what you read.

After you read a story, you usually know more than you did before. There are many ways to find out how well you understood what you read. One simple way is to answer questions.

When you are working with the ***Power Builders***, you will read the story and answer questions to check your understanding. You will write your answers on a Record Page, not on the *Power Builder*. Remember, you can always turn back to the story if you need help.

If you follow the steps we've talked about, you will probably find it easier to understand and remember what you read.

You may want to display the questions on a board or wall for students to refer to as they read the ***Power Builders.***

Power Builders: Individual Conferences

SESSION 7

Summary: Today you'll review the work individual students have been doing. One of the first things you want to find out is whether each student has been placed in the correct color and corresponding Lexile® level in ***SRA Reading Laboratory.*** The Starter Stories you administered earlier are not precise instruments, although they are a good general indicator of the best level at which a student should begin. Psychological factors, some uneasiness about working under pressure of time, or simply lucky guessing may result in better or worse performance with the Starter Stories than actual ability warrants. If this was the case, it should become apparent now as you review the student's Progress Charts, and an adjustment of the student's placement can be made.

Procedures

Once the ***Power Builder*** procedures are established, you will hold a counseling session with each student. While the class is working with ***Power Builders*** or doing free reading, begin conferences with individual students. Ask a student to come to your desk, bringing along his or her latest Progress Chart. Begin by asking the student how he or she is doing and how he or she is enjoying the work. Then examine the Progress Chart. If you have any questions about how accurately the chart reflects the student's true abilities, he or she should read to you from one of the ***Power Builders*** so you can make a more direct assessment.

To the greatest extent possible, your student conferences should be cooperative ventures in which you and the student reach a decision together regarding the student's performance. The student should be encouraged to help decide whether he or she is ready to advance to a new level, or whether remaining in the current level for a while longer is appropriate. Students unused to having such responsibility for their own instruction and progress will probably be a little hesitant to join in the decision at first. Soon, however, they will become accustomed to the idea and will acquire considerable skill in analyzing their work.

Individual development and progress is the goal.

In these conferences, students may reveal certain concerns. They may feel ashamed to make mistakes. If so, explain that it is natural to make mistakes and that mistakes can help you learn, provided you take the time to find out why you made the mistake.

Students may be worried because of the irregular appearance–highs and lows–of their Progress Charts. Explain that there is no perfect progress from day to day. The important thing is the general direction in which they are moving.

Students may be worried about competition with others. Emphasize that students develop at different rates. The important thing is each student's development. Students who advance through the lower levels make as much progress as those who advance through the higher levels.

Advancing to a Higher Color Level

It is during these student conferences that you will consider whether students are ready to move to a higher color level. During the program, some students can be expected to advance three, four, or even five color levels.

Generally, a typical student should complete four to six ***Power Builders*** and achieve scores of eighty percent or higher in both the Build Comprehension and the Learn about Words sections before moving to a higher color level. Some students may need to finish all the ***Power Builders*** before moving to a new color level.

Occasionally, students will not want to advance because they enjoy the success they are having with the easier work. Then you will have to prod them a little. On the other hand, there are always a few students who are too anxious to advance. You will tactfully have to slow their progress without destroying their enthusiasm. In either case, the Progress Charts are the basis for wise decisions.

Interpreting Progress Charts

If a student is not moving smoothly through a color level—improving scores steadily—review the Progress Charts with the Comprehension and Word-Study Skills Chart for that color level. On the next page is a sample of a typical Progress Chart. A study of this chart will help you guide students in evaluating their own work and programming their own learning.

1 The student has been working at the Orange Level. Her Progress Chart shows that she has read Orange ***Power Builders*** 12, 3, 1, 4, and 9.

2 Look at the Build Comprehension section on the sample Progress Chart. You see that only in ***Power Builder*** 4 has she scored below eighty percent. She missed Questions 3 and 4, which involve comparing and contrasting according to the sample Orange Level Comprehension and Word-Study Skills Chart.

The Comprehension and Word-Study Skills Chart shows that ***Power Builders*** 1, 8, and 11 will give the student further practice in comparing and contrasting.

3 You also notice that the student has had difficulty with Learn about Words. Her Record Pages show that her problem lies in Section C, using words in context. ***Power Builders*** 1, 8, and 11 will not only help her with comparing and contrasting (Section A) but will give her practice in using words.

4 Naturally, you will not simply assign additional ***Power Builders;*** you will want to model and reteach as necessary. You will want to discuss all problem areas with the students. You may find that low scores in a particular section are a matter of having misunderstood the directions for that section. Remind students to look back at incorrect answers to see why they missed them and to discuss them with you if they still don't understand.

Use the Progress Charts to help you differentiate instruction if needed.

My Reading Progress Chart: Orange Level

Fill in the box for each correct answer on your Power Builder.

Power Builder Number	Date	A Build Comprehension	B C Learn about Words	D Focus on Skills
12	Oct. 9	1 2 3 4 5	1 2 3 4 5 6 7 8 9 10	1 2 3 4 5
3	Oct. 11	1 2 3 4 5	1 2 3 4 5 6 7 8 9 10	1 2 3 4 5
1	Oct. 13	1 2 3 4 5	1 2 3 4 5 6 7 8 9 10	1 2 3 4 5
4	Oct. 16	1 2 3 4 5	1 2 3 4 5 6 7 8 9 10	1 2 3 4 5
9	Oct. 19	1 2 3 4 5	1 2 3 4 5 6 7 8 9 10	1 2 3 4 5
		1 2 3 4 5	1 2 3 4 5 6 7 8 9 10	1 2 3 4 5
		1 2 3 4 5	1 2 3 4 5 6 7 8 9 10	1 2 3 4 5
		1 2 3 4 5	1 2 3 4 5 6 7 8 9 10	1 2 3 4 5
		1 2 3 4 5	1 2 3 4 5 6 7 8 9 10	1 2 3 4 5
		1 2 3 4 5	1 2 3 4 5 6 7 8 9 10	1 2 3 4 5
		1 2 3 4 5	1 2 3 4 5 6 7 8 9 10	1 2 3 4 5
		1 2 3 4 5	1 2 3 4 5 6 7 8 9 10	1 2 3 4 5

Orange	Power Builder Number											
	1	2	3	4	5	6	7	8	9	10	11	12
A Build Comprehension	Item Numbers											
Identifying the Main Idea	1	1	1	1	1	1	1	1	1	1	1	1
Drawing Conclusions	5	2, 4	2	5	3	2, 3, 4		3, 5	5	2, 3, 4		4
Making Inferences			3		2, 4		2, 3, 4	2	2, 3, 4			
Understanding Cause and Effect	2		4								2, 3	
Comparing and Contrasting	3, 4			2, 3, 4				4			4	
Predicting Outcomes		5	5		5		5			5	5	5
Identifying Literary Elements		3				5						2, 3
Learn about Words												
B Minimal-Contrast Word Building	ay	ake	ill	ing	at	ay	an	ake	ick	ot	ight	all
C Using Words in Context	●	●	●	●	●	●	●	●	●	●	●	●
Focus on Skills												
Descriptive Language	D				D						D	
Giving Reasons				D				D		D		
Pronoun Antecedents		D					D					D
Rhyming Words			D			D			D			

Final Evaluation

SESSION 8

Summary: When your class has finished *Power Builders* for the year, lead a class discussion of what they have learned about reading and what they have enjoyed about *SRA Reading Laboratory*. Careful attention to students' comments can help you identify ways to work more effectively with individuals and the class as a whole.

Procedures

Encourage students to tell a little about their favorite story or to tell something new and interesting they learned from reading the *Power Builders*. Try to make sure each student who wants to share something has a chance to do so.

Review the comprehension strategy lessons. Ask students how they have used the strategies in their other classwork. Ask them to share any other ways in which their *Power Builder* work has helped with other reading they have done.

Encourage students to apply the strategies they have learned in their other classwork.

Remind students to continue using the techniques and strategies they have learned as they read, both for reading textbooks and for pleasure reading.

References and Resources

APPENDIX A: Answers to Frequently Asked Questions

When should SRA Reading Laboratory *be started?*

Teachers generally find it most desirable to schedule *SRA Reading Laboratory* work as early as possible in the school year. The increased reading efficiency built by the program can then be put to use in all school subjects for the greater part of the school year.

Why not widely space the program practice?

Wide spacing between sessions is not recommended because the principle of reinforcement does not operate well when the program sessions are spaced far apart. When practice periods are close together, there is a carryover of learning from one day to the next. When practice periods are too far apart, there is greater risk that students will forget both the information learned and the procedures to follow. During the early stages of a learning process, practice is most efficient when closely spaced.

What about grading?

It is recommended that a student's work in the program be ungraded; the Progress Charts should tell the story. If students are reading successfully at a low level but working up to their ability, is it fair to give them a poor grade? On the other hand, such students should not be led to consider themselves above average only to find later that they are deficient in academic ability. If a grade is necessary, a dual grading system might be used–one grade for effort and another for realistic ranking of functional ability. Such a system might prove useful not only for below-grade-level students but also for above-grade-level students who do only average work because of lack of effort.

What determines the difficulty of the color levels?

A Lexile® range has been assigned to each color level, with the Lexile® range increasing for each subsequent color. An official Lexile® score has been assigned to each reading passage. Then the reading passage has been placed in the appropriate color level based on the Lexile® score. In addition, the length of the reading selections increases at every level, and the comprehension checks and word study exercises become more mechanically complex and demand increasingly sophisticated kinds of thinking.

See the chart below for the reading level and Lexile® range for each color level in the 1c ***SRA Reading Laboratory.***

COLOR LEVEL	APPROXIMATE READING LEVEL	LEXILE® RANGE
Orange	1.6	290L–340L
Gold	1.8	340L–390L
Brown	2.0	390L–440L
Tan	2.2	440L–490L
Lime	2.4	490L–540L
Green	2.6	540L–590L
Olive	2.8	590L–640L
Aqua	3.0	640L–690L
Blue	3.5	690L–740L
Purple	4.0	740L–790L
Violet	4.5	790–840L
Rose	5.0	840L–890L

What about competition and cheating?

Competition and cheating are closely interrelated problems. If a student takes advantage of the *Key Cards'* availability to copy answers or if the student otherwise falsifies his or her scores, it is probably done in an effort to keep up with other class members or to get ahead of them.

For this reason, it is important in the initial stages of the program to convey the idea that multilevel work does not involve a race among classmates—that different students will be in different color levels because students differ, and this program provides materials that are appropriate for each one.

It is also important to minimize the idea that moving from one color level to another is the badge of success. This is *one kind* of success, which might be called vertical progress. But there is also horizontal progress—success in each ***Power Builder*** a student completes within a level. Each ***Power Builder*** presents new skills to master or different approaches to similar skills. Students should, therefore, be encouraged to see their goal as one of simply working as well as possible with the materials that are appropriate for them. They should not view climbing up the ladder of color levels as the only goal of their work. Obviously, you must play a key role in forming appropriate attitudes about what constitutes success.

Students hurt only themselves when they seek status among classmates by defeating the program's continuous placement mechanism and by moving ahead in the color sequence by means of copied answers or falsified scores. Those students miss needed practice and encounter material that is too difficult. You can try to communicate this idea, although obviously there will be resistance if a student has been taunted by a classmate for being "only in Orange," for example. You then face the traditional problem of how to motivate a student to do what's best in the long run when the student prefers to do what seems to provide immediate status and peer acceptance. It is a problem that occurs in all areas of student behavior when a competitive atmosphere exists, and it is by no means a unique problem to this program. Teachers who have found ways to remedy this problem in other areas of school life will probably handle it successfully in connection with this program.

If cheating is apparent, a confidential talk with the student is a good idea. You can stress the idea that "one only cheats oneself" and help the student understand that hurrying from level to level is not the aim of the program. Remember, too, that by spot-checking for errors and by praising accuracy and neatness in scoring, calculating, and charting, you can set up an atmosphere that discourages cheating.

Finally, remember that it is *not* cheating for students to look back at the story in order to answer the comprehension and vocabulary checks. Indeed, looking back should be encouraged as preferable to guessing or relying on uncertain recollections. Looking back is what we all do (and *should* do) in real-life reading situations when we want to be sure about what we have read. Once this is understood, some students may no longer have the need to misuse the ***Key Card*** or alter their scores.

What about record keeping?

Because *SRA Reading Laboratory* is student directed, you enter no scores and correct no papers. Each student keeps all the necessary records on the Record Pages and the Progress Charts. The records each student maintains are invaluable guides to the diagnosis of his or her reading difficulties, progress, and long-range educational potential.

The value of these student-kept records is threefold:

(1) In parent conferences, the Progress Charts form an objective basis for interpreting school progress in the vital area of reading. They provide a direct and unbiased reflection of the student's day-to-day work.

(2) In student guidance, the Progress Charts represent a cumulative record of the student's actual *functional* ability to learn through reading. Such information is useful in helping both the parent and the teacher or guidance worker—as well as the student—in realistically planning the student's educational future.

(3) In curriculum improvement, analysis of the functional reading levels of pupils may indicate to the teacher or curriculum worker a need for revising upward or downward the difficulty level of offerings in the various subject areas. Such a study might point out a need for further steps toward individualizing learning opportunities.

APPENDIX B: Power Builder Titles

Level	Title	Word Count	LEXILE®
Orange	**Lexile® Range 290L–340L**		
1	*The Clouds*	108	300L
2	*The Wish*	111	330L
3	*Jinx's Tooth*	107	340L
4	*How Birds Talk*	119	340L
5	*Lovely Nina*	94	340L
6	*Shirley and the Boy*	108	300L
7	*Fire!*	100	310L
8	*Where Plants Grow*	98	340L
9	*A Magic Stick*	109	300L
10	*A Brother's Trick*	100	340L
11	*Night Lights in the Ocean*	103	310L
12	*Toys for Sale*	105	340L
Gold	**Lexile® Range 340L–390L**		
1	*Sam and Mr. Stone*	129	390L
2	*Jay's Homework*	121	390L
3	*Fire Watch*	122	350L
4	*Day Owl, Night Owl*	131	340L
5	*Nate's Mystery*	126	380L
6	*Cats*	121	380L
7	*A Nature Adventure*	143	340L
8	*Ten in a Pen*	161	360L
9	*Dinosaur Eggs*	136	380L
10	*Animals in the Woods*	136	370L
11	*Good Friends*	154	340L
12	*Language of the Bees*	140	370L

Appendix B

Level	Title	Word Count	LEXILE®
Brown	**Lexile® Range 390L–440L**		
1	*The New Food Adventure*	162	420L
2	*Gerri's Horn*	159	440L
3	*That Surprising Animal*	164	430L
4	*I Love Tennis*	155	440L
5	*What's for Breakfast?*	185	440L
6	*Energy*	160	440L
7	*The New Playground*	157	440L
8	*The Good Luck Clothes*	147	410L
9	*The Ants and the Grasshopper*	152	390L
10	*Shadow Friends*	176	410L
11	*Hal and Max*	150	440L
12	*Weather and Seasons*	172	440L
Tan	**Lexile® Range 440L–490L**		
1	*Tracking a Dragon*	230	470L
2	*Notes from School*	206	470L
3	*Astronaut in the Making*	171	490L
4	*Do Fish Have Feet?*	211	460L
5	*The Cornfield*	199	440L
6	*Nita's First Camera*	215	470L
7	*Rocks*	183	470L
8	*Song of the Coyote*	180	480L
9	*The Electric Hippopotamus*	215	490L
10	*The Top of Bear Hill*	225	480L
11	*How an Airplane Flies*	220	460L
12	*The Fish Princess*	231	480L

Level	Title	Word Count	LEXILE®
Lime	**Lexile® Range 490L–540L**		
1	*Leaving Home Behind*	246	510L
2	*From Tadpole to Frog*	197	500L
3	*Learning about the Moon*	280	510L
4	*Spiders Spin Webs*	216	520L
5	*Around and Around*	221	530L
6	*Quiz*	246	540L
7	*Tiny but Tough*	192	530L
8	*The Tendon of Achilles*	226	540L
9	*Rosa's Bike*	270	500L
10	*How Do Seeds Travel?*	260	490L
11	*The Mystery Tower*	211	520L
12	*How Hard Can the Wind Blow?*	248	500L
Green	**Lexile® Range 540L–590L**		
1	*Raven Shows the Way*	288	540L
2	*Colors That Hide*	299	580L
3	*Pet Helpers*	221	560L
4	*Natural Resources*	301	590L
5	*Sara's First Baseball Game*	325	540L
6	*How Do You Catch a Gooey Duck?*	264	570L
7	*A Worldwide Pastime*	276	540L
8	*The Magnificent Moon*	250	560L
9	*A Colorful Hike*	251	550L
10	*The Great Epizootic*	273	590L
11	*What Are Leaves For?*	221	590L
12	*Being Responsible at School*	256	560L

Appendix B

Level	Title	Word Count	LEXILE®
Olive	**Lexile® Range 590L–640L**		
1	*Kids Make a Difference*	371	610L
2	*Hic!*	302	620L
3	*Wildfires*	345	610L
4	*The Queen's Shawl*	358	610L
5	*Cooperation Works*	388	610L
6	*The Fabulous Niagara Falls*	313	640L
7	*Night Flight*	400	620L
8	*Rain!*	324	640L
9	*Changing Weather*	369	640L
10	*The Mystery of the Missing Glove*	341	590L
11	*Sir Christopher Wren*	361	630L
12	*Making Money in America*	408	630L
Aqua	**Lexile® Range 640L–690L**		
1	*A Surprise for Scooter*	510	670L
2	*How the Cheetah Got Its Tear Stains*	380	640L
3	*Marco and the Book*	445	650L
4	*Bikes*	447	650L
5	*Angela and the Bees*	417	640
6	*Thurgood Marshall*	418	690L
7	*A Guiding Light*	380	640L
8	*The Food Chain*	432	690L
9	*Bugs in a Box*	447	640L
10	*Wildcats of the Americas*	426	640L
11	*Those Amazing Lemmings*	375	650L
12	*One of Those Days*	402	690L

Level	Title	Word Count	LEXILE®
Blue	**Lexile® Range 690L–740L**		
1	*A Trail of Destiny*	549	720L
2	*Flight 19*	522	720L
3	*20,000 Leagues Under the Sea*	506	740L
4	*Salt: It Isn't Just for Food*	444	700L
5	*Another Mighty Blast from the Babe*	577	700L
6	*Watch Out!*	496	740L
7	*The Curse of the Hope Diamond*	552	720L
8	*The King's Lesson*	573	710L
9	*Call the Firefighters*	433	720L
10	*Abuela's Room*	449	740L
11	*Behind the Mask: The Real Story of King Tut*	513	710L
12	*The Drum*	580	720L
Purple	**Lexile® Range 740L–790L**		
1	*The Storm's Surprise*	542	790L
2	*Dog Cousins*	569	780L
3	*Don't Lose Your Head!*	615	760L
4	*Passage Across a Nation*	634	780L
5	*Captain Carmen*	620	790L
6	*Otters*	507	780L
7	*The Remarkable Adventure of Sir Ernest Shackleton*	616	780L
8	*The Iditarod: Alaska's Great Race*	616	760L
9	*The Man Who Loved Himself*	608	760L
10	*The Crocodile Hunter*	581	790L
11	*Alessia's Quilt*	638	780L
12	*Trading Places*	632	790L

Appendix B

Level	Title	Word Count	LEXILE®
Violet	**Lexile® Range 790L–840L**		
1	*An AéraGames First*	649	820L
2	*The American Turkey*	575	830L
3	*The Boy, the Wagon, and the Rat*	690	790L
4	*Four Seasons*	611	830L
5	*Creatures of the Deep*	596	820L
6	*Steve Jobs*	669	790L
7	*Foolish Kailani*	668	840L
8	*The Great Houdini*	756	830L
9	*All Kinds of Toys*	654	810L
10	*Turning Bananas into Gold*	722	800L
11	*The Story of Seabiscuit*	696	800L
12	*The Monkey and the Sea Star*	714	790L
Rose	**Lexile® Range 840L–890L**		
1	*Curious Cari*	994	870L
2	*The Big Switch*	1057	840L
3	*Aaron the Actor*	681	870L
4	*Martha Mason: A Life Lived Well*	859	860L
5	*The Messy Room*	955	870L
6	*Earthquake!*	684	890L
7	*Pictures in Her Head*	835	850L
8	*Marian Anderson and Her Legacy*	727	850L
9	*Gina's Japanese Adventure*	645	840L
10	*Homesteading in the United States*	685	850L
11	*Hosting the World Cup*	773	860L
12	*Because It Is There*	713	880L

APPENDIX C: Comprehension and Word-Study Skills Charts

Orange	Power Builder Number											
	1	2	3	4	5	6	7	8	9	10	11	12
A Build Comprehension	Item Numbers											
Identifying the Main Idea	1	1	1	1	1	1	1	1	1	1	1	1
Drawing Conclusions	5	2, 4	2	5	3	2, 3, 4		3, 5	5	2, 3, 4		4
Making Inferences			3		2, 4		2, 3, 4	2	2, 3, 4			
Understanding Cause and Effect	2										2, 3	
Comparing and Contrasting	3, 4		4	2, 3, 4				4			4	
Predicting Outcomes		5	5		5		5			5	5	5
Identifying Literary Elements		3				5						2, 3
Learn about Words												
B Minimal-Contrast Word Building	ay	ake	ill	ing	at	ay	an	ake	ick	ot	ight	all
C Using Words in Context	●	●	●	●	●	●	●	●	●	●	●	●
Focus on Skills												
Descriptive Language	D				D						D	
Giving Reasons				D				D		D		
Pronoun Antecedents		D					D					D
Rhyming Words			D			D			D			

Gold	Power Builder Number											
	1	2	3	4	5	6	7	8	9	10	11	12
Ⓐ Build Comprehension	**Item Numbers**											
Identifying the Main Idea	1	1	1	1	1	1	1	1	1	1	1	1
Drawing Conclusions	4		4, 5	3	4	2, 5	5	3, 4	4, 5	5	5	4
Making Inferences				4, 5				2, 5	2		2, 3	
Understanding Cause and Effect	2, 3	3, 4, 5	2, 3	2			2		3	2, 3, 4		2, 3
Comparing and Contrasting						4						
Predicting Outcomes		2				3					4	5
Identifying Literary Elements	5				2, 3, 5		3, 4					
Learn about Words												
Ⓑ Minimal-Contrast Word Building	ad	ay	ake	ight	ing	at	ell	en	ill	ill	ad	ay
Ⓒ Using Words in Context	●	●	●	●	●	●	●	●	●	●	●	●
Focus on Skills												
Descriptive Language			D					D		D		
Synonyms		D				D			D			
Punctuation	D			D								D
Contractions					D		D				D	

Brown	Power Builder Number											
	1	2	3	4	5	6	7	8	9	10	11	12
Ⓐ Build Comprehension	Item Numbers											
Identifying the Main Idea	1	1	1	1	1	1	1	1	1	1	1	1
Drawing Conclusions			2, 3	2, 5	2	2, 3, 4	3, 5	5		3, 4	2, 4	
Making Inferences	3	4			4		4					2, 3
Understanding Cause and Effect	2, 4		5	3							5	
Comparing and Contrasting			4	4								
Predicting Outcomes	5	5				5			4, 5	5		4, 5
Identifying Literary Elements		2, 3			3, 5		2	2, 4	2, 3	2		
Recognizing Problems and Solutions								3			3	
Learn about Words												
Ⓑ Word Study												
Compound Words	●				●			●				
Regular Plurals			●			●						●
Contractions				●					●		●	
Possessives		●					●			●		
Ⓒ Using New Words in Context	●	●	●	●	●	●	●	●	●	●	●	●
Focus on Skills												
Similes			D					D		D		
Antonyms				D			D					D
Past Tense		D			D				D			
Alphabetical Order	D					D					D	

Appendix C

Tan	Power Builder Number											
	1	2	3	4	5	6	7	8	9	10	11	12
Ⓐ Build Comprehension	Item Numbers											
Identifying the Main Idea	1	1	1	1	1	1	1	1	1	1	1	1
Drawing Conclusions	5	5	2	4	2	3, 4		4	2	2	2, 5	3, 4
Making Inferences	2, 3, 4	4	5				2, 3	5				5
Understanding Cause and Effect		2		3	4		4	2, 3	3	3, 4	4	
Comparing and Contrasting			3, 4	2, 5							3	
Predicting Outcomes						5	5		5	5		
Identifying Literary Elements		3				2						2
Recognizing Problems and Solutions					3, 5				4			
Learn about Words												
Ⓑ Word Study												
Compound Words			●				●				●	
Regular Plurals		●		●				●				
Contractions	●					●				●		
Possessives					●				●			●
Ⓒ Using New Words in Context	●	●	●	●	●	●	●	●	●	●	●	●
Focus on Skills												
Predictions	D								E	E		
Story Map		D			D			D				
Topic Details				E			E				E	
Similes			D			D						D
Alphabetical Order			E			E		E				
Pronoun Antecedents		E					D			D		
Past Tense					E				D			E
Punctuation	E			D							D	

Lime	Power Builder Number											
	1	2	3	4	5	6	7	8	9	10	11	12
A Build Comprehension	Item Numbers											
Identifying the Main Idea	1	1	1	1	1	1	1	1	1	1	1	1
Drawing Conclusions	4		2, 4	3, 5	2			2	2		3, 4	2, 3, 5
Making Inferences	3	4, 5	5	2, 4	3, 5	3, 4		5	5		2	4
Understanding Cause and Effect	5	2				2, 5	4	3, 4	3, 4			
Comparing and Contrasting			3				3			2, 3		
Predicting Outcomes							5			4, 5	5	
Identifying Literary Elements					4		2					
Sequence	2	3										
Learn about Words												
B Word Meaning in Context	●	●	●	●	●	●	●	●	●	●	●	●
C Using New Words in Context	●	●	●	●	●	●	●	●	●	●	●	●
Focus on Skills												
Sequence		D			D		D					
Fact or Opinion				D				D			E	
Topic Details			E			E				E		
Antonyms	D						E		D			
Contractions		E				D						D
Blends	E			E					E			
Compound Words					E			E			D	
Punctuation			D							D		E

Green	Power Builder Number											
	1	2	3	4	5	6	7	8	9	10	11	12
A Build Comprehension	Item Numbers											
Identifying the Main Idea	1	1	1	1	1	1	1	1	1	1	1	1
Drawing Conclusions	3	2, 3, 4		2, 3	3, 4		2, 3, 4	3	2	2	2, 5	5
Making Inferences	2, 4	5	3, 4		2, 5	5	5	4, 5		4	3, 4	2
Understanding Cause and Effect			2	4, 5		3, 4		2	5	3		
Comparing and Contrasting						2						3, 4
Predicting Outcomes			5							5		
Identifying Literary Elements	5											
Recognizing Problems and Solutions									3, 4			
Learn about Words												
B Word Meaning in Context	●	●	●	●	●	●	●	●	●	●	●	●
C Using New Words in Context	●	●	●	●	●	●	●	●	●	●	●	●
Focus on Skills												
Story Structure			D		D				D			
Predictions	D							D		D		
Fact or Opinion				D		D					E	
Similes		E					D					D
Past Tense	E						E			E		
Prefixes			E			E						E
Compound Words		D		E				E				
Pronoun Antecedents					E				E		D	

Olive	Power Builder Number											
	1	2	3	4	5	6	7	8	9	10	11	12
A Build Comprehension	Item Numbers											
Identifying the Main Idea	1	1	1	1	1	1	1	1	1	1	1	1
Drawing Conclusions	4	2, 5	3, 4	4	2, 5	2, 4		2, 5		3	2	2
Making Inferences	2	4	5		3	3, 5	4			4	3, 4, 5	5
Understanding Cause and Effect			2				2, 3	3, 4	3	2, 5		
Comparing and Contrasting		3							2, 4, 5			3, 4
Predicting Outcomes							5					
Identifying Literary Elements				3, 5	4							
Recognizing Problems and Solutions	3, 5			2								
Learn about Words												
B Word Meaning in Context	●	●	●	●	●	●	●	●	●	●	●	●
C Word Relationships	●	●	●	●	●	●	●	●	●	●	●	●
Focus on Skills												
Comparisons									E			E
Anologies		E						D			D	
Similes				D		D				D		
Summarizing	D				D		E					
Suffixes		D			E		D					
Inflectional Endings	E							E		E		
Irregular Plurals			D			E						D
Dictionary Guide Words			E	E					D		E	

Aqua	Power Builder Number											
	1	2	3	4	5	6	7	8	9	10	11	12
A Build Comprehension	Item Numbers											
Identifying the Main Idea	1	1	1	1	1	1	1	1	1	1	1	1
Drawing Conclusions	4	2	2				3	2	4		2, 5	3, 4, 5
Making Inferences	3		4	4	4, 5	5	2, 4, 5	5	2, 3, 5		3, 4	
Understanding Cause and Effect	2	4		3, 5	3	3, 4		3, 4		2		2
Comparing and Contrasting		3, 5		2	2	2				3, 4		
Predicting Outcomes	5									5		
Identifying Literary Elements			3, 5									
Learn about Words												
B Word Meaning in Context	●	●	●	●	●	●	●	●	●	●	●	●
C Word Relationships	●	●	●	●	●	●	●	●	●	●	●	●
Focus on Skills												
Topic Details		E		E							E	
Comparisons					D		D			E		
Story Structure			D						D			
Fact or Opinion	D				E			D				
Past Tense	E					E					D	
Prefixes		D					E			D		
Pronouns				D		D			E			E
Contractions			E					E				D

Blue	Power Builder Number											
	1	2	3	4	5	6	7	8	9	10	11	12
A Build Comprehension	Item Numbers											
Identifying the Main Idea	1	1	1	1	1	1	1	1	1	1	1	1
Drawing Conclusions		3, 5	2, 3		2, 3		2, 3, 4		2, 4, 5		3, 5	
Making Inferences	4	4		2, 5	4, 5		5	2, 3, 5				5
Understanding Cause and Effect				3, 4				4	3	2	2, 4	4
Comparing and Contrasting		2										
Predicting Outcomes	5		5									
Identifying Literary Elements	2, 3		4			2				3, 4, 5		
Recognizing Problems and Solutions						3, 4, 5						2, 3
Learn about Words												
B Word Meaning in Context	●	●	●	●	●	●	●	●	●	●	●	●
C Word Relationships	●	●	●	●	●	●	●	●	●	●	●	●
Focus on Skills												
Story Map	D						D			D		
Character Feelings			E			E						D
Classification		D					F		D		D	
Comparisons				F					F		F	
Idioms			F			F		F				
Sequence			D		D							
Synonyms	F			E	F							
Possessive Pronouns				D	E					E		
Suffixes	E	E					E		E	F		F
Prefixes						D		D				E
Contractions		F						E			E	

Purple	**Power Builder Number**											
	1	**2**	**3**	**4**	**5**	**6**	**7**	**8**	**9**	**10**	**11**	**12**
A Build Comprehension	**Item Numbers**											
Identifying the Main Idea	1	1	1	1	1	1	1	1	1	1	1	1
Drawing Conclusions				2, 3		2	3, 5	2, 4	5	2, 5	5	4
Making Inferences	5	4, 5		4, 5	3	4		5				2, 5
Understanding Cause and Effect	2, 3, 4	2, 3	3		2, 4, 5	3, 5	2, 4	3	2	3, 4	2, 3	
Predicting Outcomes			4, 5								4	
Identifying Literary Elements			2									3
Recognizing Problems and Solutions									3, 4			
Learn about Words												
B Word Meaning in Context	●	●	●	●	●	●	●	●	●	●	●	●
C Word Relationships	●	●	●	●	●	●	●	●	●	●	●	●
Focus on Skills												
Classification		E, F				E		D			F	E
Exact Words				F				E			E	
Story Map			F				D			D		
Sequence	D				E							D
Topic Details	F					F		F				
Fact or Opinion				D		D				E		
Suffixes	E				F				F			
Possessive Pronouns			E				E					F
Comparatives and Superlatives			D						D		D	
Articles				E			F			F		
Antonyms		D			D				E			

Violet	Power Builder Number											
	1	2	3	4	5	6	7	8	9	10	11	12
A Build Comprehension	Item Numbers											
Identifying the Main Idea	1	1	1	1	1	1	1	1	1	1	1	1
Drawing Conclusions				3	2, 4, 5	2		4	2, 4			
Making Inferences	4, 5	3, 4	4, 5	4		3	5	5	3, 5	2	5	
Understanding Cause and Effect	3	2	2, 3		3					4		2
Comparing and Contrasting	2	5				4					3, 4	
Predicting Outcomes				5		5				3, 5		
Identifying Literary Elements				2			2, 3, 4				2	3, 4, 5
Recognizing Problems and Solutions								2, 3				
Learn about Words												
B Word Meaning in Context	●	●	●	●	●	●	●	●	●	●	●	●
C Word Relationships	●	●	●	●	●	●	●	●	●	●	●	●
Focus on Skills												
Classification		E						D			E	
Comparisons		D				D			D			
Metaphors						E		E				F
Idioms	F			E						E		
Homophones	D						E					E
Editing: Redundancy			E				D			F		
Character Feelings			D								D	D
Onomatopoeia			F			F				D		
Irregular Past Tense		F			F				E			
Suffixes	E			F	D							
Possessive Pronouns				D			F		F			
Articles					E			F			F	

Rose	Power Builder Number											
	1	2	3	4	5	6	7	8	9	10	11	12
Ⓐ Build Comprehension	Item Numbers											
Identifying the Main Idea	1	1	1	1	1	1	1	1	1	1	1	1
Drawing Conclusions	2			4		5		4, 5		5	2	3, 5
Making Inferences		5		5			3, 5	2	4, 5	4		
Understanding Cause and Effect	4	2, 3, 4	4			2, 3		3				2, 4
Comparing and Contrasting				2, 3		4			3	2, 3	3, 4	
Predicting Outcomes					5						5	
Identifying Literary Elements	3		2, 3, 5		2, 3, 4		2, 4		2			
Recognizing Problems and Solutions	5											
Learn about Words												
Ⓑ Word Meaning in Context	●	●	●	●	●	●	●	●	●	●	●	●
Ⓒ Word Relationships	●	●	●	●	●	●	●	●	●	●	●	●
Focus on Skills												
Exact Words					E							F
Idioms			E			E		E	E			
Simile/Metaphor	E			E							D	
Homophones			D	D					F			
Editing: Redundancy		D						F		D		
Story Map	D				D		D					
Onomatopoeia		E						D			E	
Irregular Past Tense	F			F					D			
Prefixes		F				F						E
Sentences: Simple/Compound			F				F			F		
Comparatives and Superlatives					F		E				F	
Pronouns						D				E		D

Student Resources

The following section contains resources for your students. You will copy and distribute these materials as needed. These resources include:

- Home Connection Letter–As you begin ***SRA Reading Laboratory*** with your students, copy the home connection letter and distribute it to students to take home and share with their parents or guardians.
- Starter Stories–These stories will be used to determine the color level at which each student should enter the ***Power Builder*** component.
- Record Page–Students write their answers to the ***Power Builder*** questions on these pages.
- Progress Charts–These allow students and you to track their progress as they work through the ***Power Builders***.

Ordering SRA Reading Laboratory® Student Record Books

In place of using the materials in the Student Resources section, keep students organized with their own individual books. Students can use their books to record answers to questions, correct their work, and record their scores and progress, promoting student accountability and ownership. To order printed copies of the Student Record Book, please visit: **https://www.mheducation.com/prek-12/explore/create-easy-order.** You can quickly find the appropriate level Student Record Book by searching for ISBN 9781309122037.

Home Connection Letter

This school year your child will be using the ***SRA Reading Laboratory*** program. This multileveled system of individualized instruction will provide your child with reading practice.

SRA Reading Laboratory offers high-interest fiction and nonfiction reading passages that cover a wide range of topics. The reading passages are divided into levels. Each level is represented by a different color, and each color is more difficult to read than the previous color.

Your child will move through the levels at his or her own pace, while working toward the following goals:

- To develop comprehension, vocabulary, word analysis, and study skills
- To reinforce specific skills to help your child become a proficient reader
- To interest your child in reading and to enlarge his or her specific knowledge, using a wide array of quality fiction and nonfiction selections
- To develop as an independent reader with strong comprehension skills, endurance, and confidence
- To develop the sense of personal responsibility by taking charge of his or her own learning

Millions of students have been using and enjoying ***SRA Reading Laboratory*** over the years. I'm sure your child will enjoy it too.

The Crow and the Crocodile

Crow and Crocodile found a big cake.

"Let's share it," said Crow.

"Let's sleep first," said Crow. "The one who has the best dream gets the cake."

Crocodile went to sleep, but Crow didn't. She ate the cake while Crocodile slept, and then she pretended to be asleep.

Crocodile woke up.

"What did you dream about?" Crow asked.

"I was eating a big dinner," said Crocodile.

Crow said, "I dreamed about food, too, but I didn't get to eat any of it. So, I ate the cake."

"Wait, you woke up and ate the cake?" shouted Crocodile.

Crow said, "You dreamed about eating that big dinner."

Crocodile laughed. "All right. But next time I get the cake and you have the dream."

Build Comprehension

A **Read each question. Write *a* or *b*.**

1. What is funny about this story?
   a. The way Crow gets all the cake
   b. The way Crocodile gets his dinner
2. Why does Crocodile go to sleep?
   a. Because he wants the cake
   b. Because he is very tired
3. Why does Crow *not* go to sleep?
   a. So Crocodile will have to share
   b. So she can eat all the cake
4. What does Crocodile eat?
   a. Crocodile eats a big dinner.
   b. Crocodile doesn't eat anything.
5. Why does Crocodile laugh?
   a. Because Crow's trick is funny
   b. Because Crow's dream is silly

Learn about Words

B sl + **ow** = **slow**

Look at each row of letters. Add one letter or group of letters from each row to *ow* to make a word. Write the word.

1. gr, dr, sr
2. wh, tr, kn
3. cl, sn, sm   + **ow**
4. d, r, j
5. qu, cr, gh

→

Learn about Words (continued)

C **Read the words you wrote. Which one best fits in each sentence? Write the word.**

6. They didn't _______ where the cake came from.
7. "Did it _______ out of the ground?" he asked.
8. "Maybe it fell out of the sky," said _______.
9. The white frosting on the cake looks like _______.
10. The cake had a _______ of pink roses on it.

Focus on Skills

D **Read the sentences. Which answer tells what *it* means? Write *a* or *b*.**

1. Crow found a cake under a tree. She wanted to share *it* with Crocodile. *It* means
   a. a tree. **b.** a cake.
2. Crocodile thought the frosting looked like snow. He liked it. *It* means
   a. the frosting. **b.** snow.
3. Crocodile had a dream when he took a nap. He told Crow about it. *It* means
   a. a nap. **b.** a dream.
4. "I had a dream about a big dinner. I ate *it* all," Crocodile said. *It* means
   a. a big dinner. **b.** a dream.
5. Crow played a trick when she ate the cake. Crocodile thought *it* was funny. *It* means
   a. a trick **b.** the cake.

A Bear's Life
Lynn_Bystrom/iStockphoto/Getty Images

It's summer. You are playing ball. The black bear is looking for food.

It's winter. You are building a snow fort. What is the black bear doing? It's sleeping.

That's the cycle of a bear's life.

In summer it looks for food. It eats fish, small animals, and some plants.

When the leaves fall, there is more food. The bear eats fruit and nuts. It gets fat. The fat will come in handy when winter comes.

Then the bear makes its winter home. It digs a big hole under a tree. It goes inside to sleep. It doesn't need food then. It uses its fat to keep warm.

When spring comes, the bear leaves the hole. Summer is coming again!

Build Comprehension

A Read each question. Write *a* or *b*.

1. What is this story about?
   a. What black bears do in summer and winter
   b. The games children play in summer and winter
2. How long does a bear sleep?
   a. A bear sleeps all winter long.
   b. A bear sleeps all summer long.
3. Why does a bear eat so much in the summer?
   a. Because there isn't much food, and it is always hungry
   b. Because it needs to be fat when winter comes
4. Why can a bear stay in a hole all winter long?
   a. Because it takes fish and nuts into its hole
   b. Because its fat keeps it full and warm
5. What will a bear most likely do when it leaves its hole in the spring?
   a. It will go to sleep.
   b. It will look for food.

Learn about Words

B b + **at** = bat

Look at each row of letters. Add one letter or group of letters from each row to *at* to make a word. Write the word.

1. gr, m, tr
2. th, cr, cl
3. qu, f, d
4. z, g, s
5. c, j, l

\+ **at**

Learn about Words (continued)

C Read the words you wrote. Which one best fits in each sentence? Write the word.

6. The bear _______ down next to its hole.
7. A _______ doesn't sleep as long as a bear does.
8. The bear eats all the food _______ it can find.
9. It needs to get _______ before winter comes.
10. The bear sleeps on a _______ of dry leaves.

Focus on Skills

D Read each sentence. If the sentence tells why a bear sleeps in its hole all winter, write *Yes.* If it does not tell why a bear sleeps in its hole all winter, write *No.*

1. A bear digs a hole under a tree.
2. There is not much food for a bear to eat in the winter.
3. A bear likes fish.
4. A hole helps a bear stay warm.
5. A bear looks for fruit and nuts.

Running

Mariam and Duane ran a race. Duane did not expect Mariam to come in first place.

"How did you run so quickly?" Duane asked.

"I run every day with my mother," Mariam said. "We go out before breakfast to run around the park."

"Can you keep up with your mother?" Duane asked.

"Yes, but I don't run for as long as she does," Mariam said. "When I get tired, I turn around and run home. Mother usually runs two miles without stopping, so I wait for her at home. Once she gets back, we have breakfast."

"That's a good idea," Duane said.

Mariam said, "Every day I run farther and faster. And, every day I get stronger. It feels good to notice the improvements."

"I'm going to start," Duane said. "I'll run every day, so I can get faster. Then we'll have another race.

Build Comprehension

A Read each question. Write *a* or *b*.

1. What does Duane find out in this story?
   a. Growing bigger will make him a better runner
   b. Running every day will make him a better runner
2. Why does Mariam win the race?
   a. Because she is older than Duane
   b. Because she runs every day
3. Why does Mariam turn around before her mother?
   a. Mariam's mother is stronger than she is
   b. Mariam wants to eat her breakfast alone
4. What does running every day do for Mariam?
   a. It makes her strong.
   b. It makes her big.
5. What does Duane think after he talks to Mariam?
   a. That he will work hard to be a better runner
   b. That he doesn't want to be a runner after all

Learn about Words

B Words change spelling when they mean more than one.

One book → two books

Write each word below so it means more than one.

1. race
2. park
3. mile
4. improvement
5. question

→

Learn about Words (continued)

C Read the new words you wrote. Which word best fits in each sentence? Write the word.

6. Duane likes to run at different ________ for a variety.
7. Exercising every day will add ________ to your performance.
8. Duane had many ________ for Mariam.
9. Mariam and Duane will face each other in many more ________.
10. How many ________ do you run in one week?

Focus on Skills

D **Word pictures help you see things more clearly. They tell you more about a story. Choose the sentence that gives a better picture. Write *a* or *b*.**

1. a. Duane is older than Mariam.
   b. Duane is two years older than Mariam.
2. a. Mariam and her mother run many places.
   b. Mariam and her mother run by the park and school.
3. a. They have toast and milk after they run.
   b. They have some breakfast after they run.
4. a. Duane wears his play clothes to the park.
   b. Duane wears shorts and running shoes to the park.
5. a. Mariam can run like the wind.
   b. Mariam can run very fast.

A Funny Way to Become Famous

1 About one hundred years ago, there was a teacher named William Archibald Spooner.

2 When he spoke, he scrambled his words. He would say the first part of one word, and then he would add the last part of another word to it.

3 Once he scolded a student for loafing. He meant to say, "You have wasted two terms." But he said, "You have tasted two worms."

4 William Spooner became famous for the way he spoke. If you say honey fat when you mean funny hat, it's called a spoonerism.

5 Once a man was selling produce. He called out, "Please buy my fruit! Please buy my fruit!" A little girl walked up to him, and as he looked at her, he smiled and spoke. And, do you know what he said?

6 "Please fry my boot!"

7 The child considered what he said, and then ran all the way home to tell her mother. She didn't want to fry boots for the man.

8 Some people are like the man who sold fruit. They say spoonerisms. But others don't mix up their words. They talk like moo and yee.

Build Comprehension

A **Choose the best ending for each sentence. Write *a* or *b*.**

1. This story is about
   - **a.** how a fruit seller became famous.
   - **b.** how mixed-up words got a name.
2. A *spoonerism* is
   - **a.** a mixed-up way of saying things.
   - **b.** one of William Spooner's students.
3. If William Spooner were your teacher,
   - **a.** you might be confused sometimes.
   - **b.** you might have to taste worms.
4. When people use spoonerisms, they
   - **a.** are trying to be funny.
   - **b.** mean to say something else.
5. In the last line of this story, *moo* and *yee* really mean
   - **a.** mine and yours.
   - **b.** you and me.

Learn about Words

B Often you can find out the meaning of a word by seeing how it is used in a story. The other words in the story give you clues.

Find the word in the story that best fits each meaning. (A paragraph number tells you where to look.) Write the word.

1. mixed up (2)
2. yelled at (3)
3. chunks of school time (3)
4. fruits and vegetables (5)
5. thought about (7)

C **Read the words you wrote. Which one best fits in each sentence? Write the word.**

6. The Internet signal was weak, so the video looked _______.
7. Mom likes to buy seasonal _______ because it has the best price.
8. Have you _______ what we'll eat for dinner tonight?
9. My sister came home for a visit after her first two _______ were over.
10. Dad _______ our dog for rolling in the mud.

Focus on Skills

D Read each story. Write *a* or *b* to answer each question.

A little girl walked up to a man who was selling fruit. She wanted an apple. She took out some money.

1. What will the man probably do next?
   - **a.** Tell the girl to go home
   - **b.** Sell the girl an apple
2. What will the girl probably do next?
   - **a.** Pay for the apple
   - **b.** Put her money away
3. How do you know what the man and the girl will do?
   - **a.** The man was selling fruit. The girl had money to buy an apple.
   - **b.** The man didn't have any fruit. The girl didn't like apples.

Mr. Spooner handed each of his students a test. He told them to pick up their pencils and begin.

4. What will the students probably do next?
   - **a.** Take the test
   - **b.** Eat their lunches
5. How do you know what the students will do?
   - **a.** They are hungry.
   - **b.** Mr. Spooner told them to begin.

E Read each set of words. Write the word that comes first in alphabetical order.

6.	want	walked	way
7.	soon	some	sold
8.	who	what	when
9.	fry	fruit	friend
10.	said	say	same

Room for One More?

1 "It's a blistering day, so I think we should drive to the lake this afternoon," Father proclaimed.

2 "Oh, that's an excellent idea!" Mother cried. "Will you go inform the children, dear?"

3 Mother thought to herself, *there'll be Jill and Phil and Father and me, and I'll invite Aunt Mary, too. There's always room for one more.*

4 Father asked, "Phil, how does going to the lake today sound?"

5 Phil responded, "That sounds great, Dad, but Harry came over to play. Could he come, too?"

6 "Yes," said Father. "There's always room for one more. Now, will you find your sister and tell her we're preparing to go?"

7 While Harry sprinted home to collect his swimsuit, Phil searched for Jill. When he found his sister, he told her everyone was going to the lake.

8 "May my friend Annie come, too?" Jill asked.

9 "Sure, there's always room for one more," Phil replied.

10 While Phil went to find his swimsuit, Annie asked Jill whether she could invite her brother, Danny.

11 "Yeah, there's always room for one more," beamed Jill.

12 Annie rushed home to grab her swimsuit and to tell her brother. Danny wanted to bring a friend, so Annie figured, *there's always room for one more.*

13 Once everyone met by the car, the pairs were Father and Mother; Jill and Phil; Aunt Mary and Harry; plus, Annie, Danny, and Danny's friend.

14 "Wow, so, there definitely isn't enough room in my car!" Father exclaimed.

15 "Well, since we all want to go," said Aunt Mary. "How about I drive my car, too? Will there be a place for me to park?"

16 Mother said, "Oh, yes, we always find a place to park."

17 "And there's always room for one more," said Father.

Build Comprehension

A Choose the best ending for each sentence. Write *a* or *b*.

1. This story shows that
   - **a.** a big family can go anywhere together.
   - **b.** a little trouble doesn't have to stop everyone's fun.
2. Lots of people are going to the lake because
   - **a.** each one asks someone else to come.
   - **b.** Mother is having a big picnic.
3. Everyone thinks there would be room for one more because
   - **a.** Mother and Father have a very large car.
   - **b.** no one knows how many people are coming.
4. When Aunt Mary says she will drive her car, too,
   - **a.** everyone gets to go to the lake.
   - **b.** there still isn't room for everyone.
5. The funny part of this story is
   - **a.** there really is room for *one* more person.
   - **b.** everyone laughs as they drive to the lake.

Learn about Words

B Often you can find out the meaning of a word by seeing how it is used in a story. The other words in the story give you clues.

Find the word in the story that best fits each meaning. (A paragraph number tells you where to look.) Write the word.

1. very hot (1)
2. said with a lot of energy (1)
3. let know (2)
4. getting ready (6)
5. thought (12)

C Read the words you wrote. Which one best fits in each sentence? Write the word.

6. Will you _______ your father that the garage door is stuck?
7. I just _______ you enjoyed sleeping in on the weekends.
8. Did you see the weather report calling for _______ heat on Saturday?
9. Mom _______ that we will go out for dinner tonight.
10. We are _______ for the snowstorm this weekend.

Focus on Skills

D The **bird's song** was as **sweet** as **honey.**

This sentence helps you understand how sweet the bird's song was. The phrase "as sweet as honey" is a **figure of speech.** It is a different way of saying that the bird's song was very lovely.

Choose the word from the first two sentences that best fits in the blank. Write the word.

1. An oven is hot. Ice is cold. It was as _______ as an oven that day.
2. A rabbit is fast. A turtle is slow. Father's car was as slow as a _______.
3. A lion is loud. A mouse is quiet. Jill was as quiet as a _______ at the lake.
4. Milk is cool. Toast is warm. That breeze is as _______ as milk.
5. Coal is black. Snow is white. Aunt Mary's hair was as _______ as snow.

E **sun + light = sunlight**

The word *sunlight* means "the light of the sun." *Sunlight* is a **compound word.**

Look at the two words in bold type. Put the two words together to complete the second sentence. Write the compound word.

6. Jill's **friend** was a **girl.** Jill invited her _______ to come over.
7. Annie brought a **suit** to **swim** in. Her _______ was red.
8. Mother's **glasses** kept the **sun** out of her eyes. She wore a pair of _______.
9. Father's **boat** had a **house** on it. Everybody went for a ride on Father's _______.
10. The **fish** Phil caught looked like a **cat.** He was proud of his _______.

Learning to Succeed

1 "The science fair is in six weeks," Mrs. Gonzalez announced. She explained how she wanted the class to choose a topic and plan out the steps of the project. Mrs. Gonzalez said the winner would get a big prize.

2 "Don't forget class," Mrs. Gonzalez said, "you need to be working steadily from now until the science fair." She wanted to make sure that students did not leave their projects until the last minute.

3 Melanie began thinking of ideas. Maybe she would study things that help plants grow. Perhaps she would investigate the moon. She even considered making a battery. In the end, Melanie decided to study shadows by making a sun dial. Ethan knew right away what he would do. He was going to do a project about airplane designs.

4 Everyone in the class submitted their ideas to Mrs. Gonzalez. She drew a big star on the calendar to show the day of the science fair. Mrs. Gonzalez reminded them that this was a big goal, and they needed to use good work habits in order to reach it.

5 Melanie was in no hurry to get started. After all, she had six weeks. Ethan, however, did not waste a minute. He made a plan for how he would complete his project. First, he would research airplanes. Then, he would test out different designs using paper airplanes. Finally, he would present all the information in a poster.

6 Each day after school, Ethan would do a little more work on his project. He made careful notes and kept the information organized. Sometimes he did not feel like working on his project after a long day at school. Even so, he made sure to do some work on it. Ethan knew he had to keep up on his plan if he wanted to achieve his goal.

7 After a few weeks, Mrs. Gonzalez asked the class how their science projects were going. Melanie started to get nervous, and she knew she had to get busy on her project. When she got home from school, however, she didn't feel like working on it. She decided to play video games instead. It wasn't like the project was due the next day. Ethan kept up his steady pace.

8 One day Mrs. Gonzalez announced, "Tomorrow is the big day. Please bring in your science projects." Ethan was happy. All he had to do was add a few finishing touches to his poster. He had completed his project and he learned a lot about airplanes. He was proud of what he had accomplished and excited that he might even win the big prize.

9 Melanie sank down in her seat. She had waited too long. There was no way she could finish her project in one night. Now she could never win the big prize. The one thing Melanie did learn was that she would need different work habits if she ever hoped to achieve her goals.

Build Comprehension

A **Choose the best ending for each sentence. Write *a, b,* or *c*.**

1. This story is about
   - **a.** winning a big prize.
   - **b.** making a sun dial.
   - **c.** working hard to achieve your goals.
2. Mrs. Gonzalez reminds the class to
   - **a.** use good work habits.
   - **b.** bring a pencil to class.
   - **c.** go to the library to research their projects.
3. Ethan is happy because
   - **a.** he played video games.
   - **b.** he completed his project.
   - **c.** he investigated the moon.
4. Melanie doesn't win the big prize because
   - **a.** she waited too long to start her project.
   - **b.** her project wasn't very good.
   - **c.** she used good work habits.
5. One way that Ethan and Melanie are different is
   - **a.** Ethan starts his project right away. Melanie waits to start her project.
   - **b.** Ethan and Melanie are in different classes.
   - **c.** Melanie likes to play video games, but Ethan doesn't.

Learn about Words

B Often you can find out the meaning of a word by seeing how it is used in a story. The other words in the story give you clues.

Find the word in the story that best fits each meaning. (A paragraph number tells you where to look.) Write the word.

1. said (1)
2. little by little (2)
3. research (3)
4. thought about (3)
5. gave (4)
6. show (5)
7. reach (6)
8. successfully completed (8)

C A word may have more than one meaning. Its meaning will depend on how it is used.

The *fly* buzzed around the room.
The bird will *fly* to its nest.

Look at each word in bold type. Note the paragraph number. Look back at the paragraph. Which meaning does the word have? Write *a* or *b*.

9. **steps** (1)
   - **a.** movements made by the foot
   - **b.** stages in a process
10. **goal** (4)
    - **a.** ambition
    - **b.** a net in a soccer game

Focus on Skills

D A story has a beginning, a middle, and an end. A story has a problem. A story is about how someone tries to solve the problem.

Parts of a Story
Beginning tells • Who • Where • The problem
Middle tells • How someone tries to solve the problem
End tells • How the problem is solved

Read each sentence. Does it tell about the beginning, the middle, or the end of the story? Write *beginning, middle,* or *end.*

1. Ethan makes a plan for his project.
2. Melanie plays video games.
3. Mrs. Gonzalez tells the class about the science fair.
4. Melanie learns that she needs different work habits.
5. Ethan decides to do his project about airplane designs.

E Some contractions are made by putting a verb and *not* together.

wasn't is made from *was not*

Other contractions are made by putting a pronoun and a verb together.

that's is made from *that is*
we'll is made from *we will*

Read each sentence. Which two words make up each underlined contraction? Write the two words.

6. Melanie <u>didn't</u> win the big prize.
7. Ethan <u>couldn't</u> believe he finished his project.
8. Mrs. Gonzalez said, "<u>Don't</u> wait until the last minute."
9. "<u>Here's</u> the details about the science fair," she said.
10. Ethan said, "<u>I'll</u> start right away."

Record Page

Name ______________________ Date __________

Power Builder Color ______________ Power Builder Number __________

(A) Build Comprehension

1. ______ 2. ______ 3. ______ 4. ______ 5. ______

Number Correct ☐

(B) (C) Learn about Words

1. ______________ 6. ______________

2. ______________ 7. ______________

3. ______________ 8. ______________

4. ______________ 9. ______________

5. ______________ 10. ______________

Number Correct ☐

(D) (E) (F) Focus on Skills

1. __________ 6. __________ 11. __________

2. __________ 7. __________ 12. __________

3. __________ 8. __________ 13. __________

4. __________ 9. __________ 14. __________

5. __________ 10. __________ 15. __________

Number Correct ☐

My Reading Progress Chart: Orange Level

Fill in the box for each correct answer on your Power Builder.

Power Builder Number	Date	A Build Comprehension	B C Learn about Words	D Focus on Skills
		1 2 3 4 5	1 2 3 4 5 6 7 8 9 10	1 2 3 4 5
		1 2 3 4 5	1 2 3 4 5 6 7 8 9 10	1 2 3 4 5
		1 2 3 4 5	1 2 3 4 5 6 7 8 9 10	1 2 3 4 5
		1 2 3 4 5	1 2 3 4 5 6 7 8 9 10	1 2 3 4 5
		1 2 3 4 5	1 2 3 4 5 6 7 8 9 10	1 2 3 4 5
		1 2 3 4 5	1 2 3 4 5 6 7 8 9 10	1 2 3 4 5
		1 2 3 4 5	1 2 3 4 5 6 7 8 9 10	1 2 3 4 5
		1 2 3 4 5	1 2 3 4 5 6 7 8 9 10	1 2 3 4 5
		1 2 3 4 5	1 2 3 4 5 6 7 8 9 10	1 2 3 4 5
		1 2 3 4 5	1 2 3 4 5 6 7 8 9 10	1 2 3 4 5
		1 2 3 4 5	1 2 3 4 5 6 7 8 9 10	1 2 3 4 5
		1 2 3 4 5	1 2 3 4 5 6 7 8 9 10	1 2 3 4 5

My Reading Progress Chart: Gold Level

Fill in the box for each correct answer on your Power Builder.

Power Builder Number	Date	Ⓐ Build Comprehension	Ⓑ Ⓒ Learn about Words	Ⓓ Focus on Skills
		1 2 3 4 5	1 2 3 4 5 6 7 8 9 10	1 2 3 4 5
		1 2 3 4 5	1 2 3 4 5 6 7 8 9 10	1 2 3 4 5
		1 2 3 4 5	1 2 3 4 5 6 7 8 9 10	1 2 3 4 5
		1 2 3 4 5	1 2 3 4 5 6 7 8 9 10	1 2 3 4 5
		1 2 3 4 5	1 2 3 4 5 6 7 8 9 10	1 2 3 4 5
		1 2 3 4 5	1 2 3 4 5 6 7 8 9 10	1 2 3 4 5
		1 2 3 4 5	1 2 3 4 5 6 7 8 9 10	1 2 3 4 5
		1 2 3 4 5	1 2 3 4 5 6 7 8 9 10	1 2 3 4 5
		1 2 3 4 5	1 2 3 4 5 6 7 8 9 10	1 2 3 4 5
		1 2 3 4 5	1 2 3 4 5 6 7 8 9 10	1 2 3 4 5
		1 2 3 4 5	1 2 3 4 5 6 7 8 9 10	1 2 3 4 5
		1 2 3 4 5	1 2 3 4 5 6 7 8 9 10	1 2 3 4 5

My Reading Progress Chart: Brown Level

Fill in the box for each correct answer on your Power Builder.

Power Builder Number	Date	A Build Comprehension	B C Learn about Words	D Focus on Skills
		1 2 3 4 5	1 2 3 4 5 6 7 8 9 10	1 2 3 4 5
		1 2 3 4 5	1 2 3 4 5 6 7 8 9 10	1 2 3 4 5
		1 2 3 4 5	1 2 3 4 5 6 7 8 9 10	1 2 3 4 5
		1 2 3 4 5	1 2 3 4 5 6 7 8 9 10	1 2 3 4 5
		1 2 3 4 5	1 2 3 4 5 6 7 8 9 10	1 2 3 4 5
		1 2 3 4 5	1 2 3 4 5 6 7 8 9 10	1 2 3 4 5
		1 2 3 4 5	1 2 3 4 5 6 7 8 9 10	1 2 3 4 5
		1 2 3 4 5	1 2 3 4 5 6 7 8 9 10	1 2 3 4 5
		1 2 3 4 5	1 2 3 4 5 6 7 8 9 10	1 2 3 4 5
		1 2 3 4 5	1 2 3 4 5 6 7 8 9 10	1 2 3 4 5
		1 2 3 4 5	1 2 3 4 5 6 7 8 9 10	1 2 3 4 5
		1 2 3 4 5	1 2 3 4 5 6 7 8 9 10	1 2 3 4 5

My Reading Progress Chart: Tan Level

Fill in the box for each correct answer on your Power Builder.

Power Builder Number	Date	A Build Comprehension	B C Learn about Words	D E Focus on Skills
		1 2 3 4 5	1 2 3 4 5 6 7 8 9 10	1 2 3 4 5 6 7 8 9 10
		1 2 3 4 5	1 2 3 4 5 6 7 8 9 10	1 2 3 4 5 6 7 8 9 10
		1 2 3 4 5	1 2 3 4 5 6 7 8 9 10	1 2 3 4 5 6 7 8 9 10
		1 2 3 4 5	1 2 3 4 5 6 7 8 9 10	1 2 3 4 5 6 7 8 9 10
		1 2 3 4 5	1 2 3 4 5 6 7 8 9 10	1 2 3 4 5 6 7 8 9 10
		1 2 3 4 5	1 2 3 4 5 6 7 8 9 10	1 2 3 4 5 6 7 8 9 10
		1 2 3 4 5	1 2 3 4 5 6 7 8 9 10	1 2 3 4 5 6 7 8 9 10
		1 2 3 4 5	1 2 3 4 5 6 7 8 9 10	1 2 3 4 5 6 7 8 9 10
		1 2 3 4 5	1 2 3 4 5 6 7 8 9 10	1 2 3 4 5 6 7 8 9 10
		1 2 3 4 5	1 2 3 4 5 6 7 8 9 10	1 2 3 4 5 6 7 8 9 10
		1 2 3 4 5	1 2 3 4 5 6 7 8 9 10	1 2 3 4 5 6 7 8 9 10
		1 2 3 4 5	1 2 3 4 5 6 7 8 9 10	1 2 3 4 5 6 7 8 9 10

My Reading Progress Chart: Lime Level

Fill in the box for each correct answer on your Power Builder.

Power Builder Number	Date	A Build Comprehension	B C Learn about Words	D E Focus on Skills
		1 2 3 4 5	1 2 3 4 5 6 7 8 9 10	1 2 3 4 5 6 7 8 9 10
		1 2 3 4 5	1 2 3 4 5 6 7 8 9 10	1 2 3 4 5 6 7 8 9 10
		1 2 3 4 5	1 2 3 4 5 6 7 8 9 10	1 2 3 4 5 6 7 8 9 10
		1 2 3 4 5	1 2 3 4 5 6 7 8 9 10	1 2 3 4 5 6 7 8 9 10
		1 2 3 4 5	1 2 3 4 5 6 7 8 9 10	1 2 3 4 5 6 7 8 9 10
		1 2 3 4 5	1 2 3 4 5 6 7 8 9 10	1 2 3 4 5 6 7 8 9 10
		1 2 3 4 5	1 2 3 4 5 6 7 8 9 10	1 2 3 4 5 6 7 8 9 10
		1 2 3 4 5	1 2 3 4 5 6 7 8 9 10	1 2 3 4 5 6 7 8 9 10
		1 2 3 4 5	1 2 3 4 5 6 7 8 9 10	1 2 3 4 5 6 7 8 9 10
		1 2 3 4 5	1 2 3 4 5 6 7 8 9 10	1 2 3 4 5 6 7 8 9 10
		1 2 3 4 5	1 2 3 4 5 6 7 8 9 10	1 2 3 4 5 6 7 8 9 10
		1 2 3 4 5	1 2 3 4 5 6 7 8 9 10	1 2 3 4 5 6 7 8 9 10

My Reading Progress Chart: Green Level

Fill in the box for each correct answer on your Power Builder.

Power Builder Number	Date	A Build Comprehension	B C Learn about Words	D E Focus on Skills
		1 2 3 4 5	1 2 3 4 5 6 7 8 9 10	1 2 3 4 5 6 7 8 9 10
		1 2 3 4 5	1 2 3 4 5 6 7 8 9 10	1 2 3 4 5 6 7 8 9 10
		1 2 3 4 5	1 2 3 4 5 6 7 8 9 10	1 2 3 4 5 6 7 8 9 10
		1 2 3 4 5	1 2 3 4 5 6 7 8 9 10	1 2 3 4 5 6 7 8 9 10
		1 2 3 4 5	1 2 3 4 5 6 7 8 9 10	1 2 3 4 5 6 7 8 9 10
		1 2 3 4 5	1 2 3 4 5 6 7 8 9 10	1 2 3 4 5 6 7 8 9 10
		1 2 3 4 5	1 2 3 4 5 6 7 8 9 10	1 2 3 4 5 6 7 8 9 10
		1 2 3 4 5	1 2 3 4 5 6 7 8 9 10	1 2 3 4 5 6 7 8 9 10
		1 2 3 4 5	1 2 3 4 5 6 7 8 9 10	1 2 3 4 5 6 7 8 9 10
		1 2 3 4 5	1 2 3 4 5 6 7 8 9 10	1 2 3 4 5 6 7 8 9 10
		1 2 3 4 5	1 2 3 4 5 6 7 8 9 10	1 2 3 4 5 6 7 8 9 10
		1 2 3 4 5	1 2 3 4 5 6 7 8 9 10	1 2 3 4 5 6 7 8 9 10

My Reading Progress Chart: Olive Level

Fill in the box for each correct answer on your Power Builder.

Power Builder Number	Date	(A) Build Comprehension	(B) (C) Learn about Words	(D) (E) Focus on Skills
		1 2 3 4 5	1 2 3 4 5 6 7 8 9 10	1 2 3 4 5 6 7 8 9 10
		1 2 3 4 5	1 2 3 4 5 6 7 8 9 10	1 2 3 4 5 6 7 8 9 10
		1 2 3 4 5	1 2 3 4 5 6 7 8 9 10	1 2 3 4 5 6 7 8 9 10
		1 2 3 4 5	1 2 3 4 5 6 7 8 9 10	1 2 3 4 5 6 7 8 9 10
		1 2 3 4 5	1 2 3 4 5 6 7 8 9 10	1 2 3 4 5 6 7 8 9 10
		1 2 3 4 5	1 2 3 4 5 6 7 8 9 10	1 2 3 4 5 6 7 8 9 10
		1 2 3 4 5	1 2 3 4 5 6 7 8 9 10	1 2 3 4 5 6 7 8 9 10
		1 2 3 4 5	1 2 3 4 5 6 7 8 9 10	1 2 3 4 5 6 7 8 9 10
		1 2 3 4 5	1 2 3 4 5 6 7 8 9 10	1 2 3 4 5 6 7 8 9 10
		1 2 3 4 5	1 2 3 4 5 6 7 8 9 10	1 2 3 4 5 6 7 8 9 10
		1 2 3 4 5	1 2 3 4 5 6 7 8 9 10	1 2 3 4 5 6 7 8 9 10
		1 2 3 4 5	1 2 3 4 5 6 7 8 9 10	1 2 3 4 5 6 7 8 9 10

My Reading Progress Chart: Aqua Level

Fill in the box for each correct answer on your Power Builder.

Power Builder Number	Date	A Build Comprehension	B C Learn about Words	D E Focus on Skills
		1 2 3 4 5	1 2 3 4 5 6 7 8 9 10	1 2 3 4 5 6 7 8 9 10
		1 2 3 4 5	1 2 3 4 5 6 7 8 9 10	1 2 3 4 5 6 7 8 9 10
		1 2 3 4 5	1 2 3 4 5 6 7 8 9 10	1 2 3 4 5 6 7 8 9 10
		1 2 3 4 5	1 2 3 4 5 6 7 8 9 10	1 2 3 4 5 6 7 8 9 10
		1 2 3 4 5	1 2 3 4 5 6 7 8 9 10	1 2 3 4 5 6 7 8 9 10
		1 2 3 4 5	1 2 3 4 5 6 7 8 9 10	1 2 3 4 5 6 7 8 9 10
		1 2 3 4 5	1 2 3 4 5 6 7 8 9 10	1 2 3 4 5 6 7 8 9 10
		1 2 3 4 5	1 2 3 4 5 6 7 8 9 10	1 2 3 4 5 6 7 8 9 10
		1 2 3 4 5	1 2 3 4 5 6 7 8 9 10	1 2 3 4 5 6 7 8 9 10
		1 2 3 4 5	1 2 3 4 5 6 7 8 9 10	1 2 3 4 5 6 7 8 9 10
		1 2 3 4 5	1 2 3 4 5 6 7 8 9 10	1 2 3 4 5 6 7 8 9 10
		1 2 3 4 5	1 2 3 4 5 6 7 8 9 10	1 2 3 4 5 6 7 8 9 10

My Reading Progress Chart: Blue Level

Fill in the box for each correct answer on your Power Builder.

Power Builder Number	Date	Ⓐ Build Comprehension	Ⓑ Ⓒ Learn about Words	Ⓓ Ⓔ Ⓕ Focus on Skills
		1 2 3 4 5	1 2 3 4 5 6 7 8 9 10	1 2 3 4 5 6 7 8 9 10 11 12 13 14 15
		1 2 3 4 5	1 2 3 4 5 6 7 8 9 10	1 2 3 4 5 6 7 8 9 10 11 12 13 14 15
		1 2 3 4 5	1 2 3 4 5 6 7 8 9 10	1 2 3 4 5 6 7 8 9 10 11 12 13 14 15
		1 2 3 4 5	1 2 3 4 5 6 7 8 9 10	1 2 3 4 5 6 7 8 9 10 11 12 13 14 15
		1 2 3 4 5	1 2 3 4 5 6 7 8 9 10	1 2 3 4 5 6 7 8 9 10 11 12 13 14 15
		1 2 3 4 5	1 2 3 4 5 6 7 8 9 10	1 2 3 4 5 6 7 8 9 10 11 12 13 14 15
		1 2 3 4 5	1 2 3 4 5 6 7 8 9 10	1 2 3 4 5 6 7 8 9 10 11 12 13 14 15
		1 2 3 4 5	1 2 3 4 5 6 7 8 9 10	1 2 3 4 5 6 7 8 9 10 11 12 13 14 15
		1 2 3 4 5	1 2 3 4 5 6 7 8 9 10	1 2 3 4 5 6 7 8 9 10 11 12 13 14 15
		1 2 3 4 5	1 2 3 4 5 6 7 8 9 10	1 2 3 4 5 6 7 8 9 10 11 12 13 14 15
		1 2 3 4 5	1 2 3 4 5 6 7 8 9 10	1 2 3 4 5 6 7 8 9 10 11 12 13 14 15
		1 2 3 4 5	1 2 3 4 5 6 7 8 9 10	1 2 3 4 5 6 7 8 9 10 11 12 13 14 15

My Reading Progress Chart: Purple Level

Fill in the box for each correct answer on your Power Builder.

Power Builder Number	Date	Ⓐ Build Comprehension	Ⓑ Ⓒ Learn about Words	Ⓓ Ⓔ Ⓕ Focus on Skills
		1 2 3 4 5	1 2 3 4 5 6 7 8 9 10	1 2 3 4 5 6 7 8 9 10 11 12 13 14 15
		1 2 3 4 5	1 2 3 4 5 6 7 8 9 10	1 2 3 4 5 6 7 8 9 10 11 12 13 14 15
		1 2 3 4 5	1 2 3 4 5 6 7 8 9 10	1 2 3 4 5 6 7 8 9 10 11 12 13 14 15
		1 2 3 4 5	1 2 3 4 5 6 7 8 9 10	1 2 3 4 5 6 7 8 9 10 11 12 13 14 15
		1 2 3 4 5	1 2 3 4 5 6 7 8 9 10	1 2 3 4 5 6 7 8 9 10 11 12 13 14 15
		1 2 3 4 5	1 2 3 4 5 6 7 8 9 10	1 2 3 4 5 6 7 8 9 10 11 12 13 14 15
		1 2 3 4 5	1 2 3 4 5 6 7 8 9 10	1 2 3 4 5 6 7 8 9 10 11 12 13 14 15
		1 2 3 4 5	1 2 3 4 5 6 7 8 9 10	1 2 3 4 5 6 7 8 9 10 11 12 13 14 15
		1 2 3 4 5	1 2 3 4 5 6 7 8 9 10	1 2 3 4 5 6 7 8 9 10 11 12 13 14 15
		1 2 3 4 5	1 2 3 4 5 6 7 8 9 10	1 2 3 4 5 6 7 8 9 10 11 12 13 14 15
		1 2 3 4 5	1 2 3 4 5 6 7 8 9 10	1 2 3 4 5 6 7 8 9 10 11 12 13 14 15
		1 2 3 4 5	1 2 3 4 5 6 7 8 9 10	1 2 3 4 5 6 7 8 9 10 11 12 13 14 15

My Reading Progress Chart: Violet Level

Fill in the box for each correct answer on your Power Builder.

Power Builder Number	Date	A Build Comprehension	B C Learn about Words	D E F Focus on Skills
		1 2 3 4 5	1 2 3 4 5 6 7 8 9 10	1 2 3 4 5 6 7 8 9 10 11 12 13 14 15
		1 2 3 4 5	1 2 3 4 5 6 7 8 9 10	1 2 3 4 5 6 7 8 9 10 11 12 13 14 15
		1 2 3 4 5	1 2 3 4 5 6 7 8 9 10	1 2 3 4 5 6 7 8 9 10 11 12 13 14 15
		1 2 3 4 5	1 2 3 4 5 6 7 8 9 10	1 2 3 4 5 6 7 8 9 10 11 12 13 14 15
		1 2 3 4 5	1 2 3 4 5 6 7 8 9 10	1 2 3 4 5 6 7 8 9 10 11 12 13 14 15
		1 2 3 4 5	1 2 3 4 5 6 7 8 9 10	1 2 3 4 5 6 7 8 9 10 11 12 13 14 15
		1 2 3 4 5	1 2 3 4 5 6 7 8 9 10	1 2 3 4 5 6 7 8 9 10 11 12 13 14 15
		1 2 3 4 5	1 2 3 4 5 6 7 8 9 10	1 2 3 4 5 6 7 8 9 10 11 12 13 14 15
		1 2 3 4 5	1 2 3 4 5 6 7 8 9 10	1 2 3 4 5 6 7 8 9 10 11 12 13 14 15
		1 2 3 4 5	1 2 3 4 5 6 7 8 9 10	1 2 3 4 5 6 7 8 9 10 11 12 13 14 15
		1 2 3 4 5	1 2 3 4 5 6 7 8 9 10	1 2 3 4 5 6 7 8 9 10 11 12 13 14 15
		1 2 3 4 5	1 2 3 4 5 6 7 8 9 10	1 2 3 4 5 6 7 8 9 10 11 12 13 14 15

My Reading Progress Chart: Rose Level

Fill in the box for each correct answer on your Power Builder.

Power Builder Number	Date	A Build Comprehension	B C Learn about Words	D E F Focus on Skills
		1 2 3 4 5	1 2 3 4 5 6 7 8 9 10	1 2 3 4 5 6 7 8 9 10 11 12 13 14 15
		1 2 3 4 5	1 2 3 4 5 6 7 8 9 10	1 2 3 4 5 6 7 8 9 10 11 12 13 14 15
		1 2 3 4 5	1 2 3 4 5 6 7 8 9 10	1 2 3 4 5 6 7 8 9 10 11 12 13 14 15
		1 2 3 4 5	1 2 3 4 5 6 7 8 9 10	1 2 3 4 5 6 7 8 9 10 11 12 13 14 15
		1 2 3 4 5	1 2 3 4 5 6 7 8 9 10	1 2 3 4 5 6 7 8 9 10 11 12 13 14 15
		1 2 3 4 5	1 2 3 4 5 6 7 8 9 10	1 2 3 4 5 6 7 8 9 10 11 12 13 14 15
		1 2 3 4 5	1 2 3 4 5 6 7 8 9 10	1 2 3 4 5 6 7 8 9 10 11 12 13 14 15
		1 2 3 4 5	1 2 3 4 5 6 7 8 9 10	1 2 3 4 5 6 7 8 9 10 11 12 13 14 15
		1 2 3 4 5	1 2 3 4 5 6 7 8 9 10	1 2 3 4 5 6 7 8 9 10 11 12 13 14 15
		1 2 3 4 5	1 2 3 4 5 6 7 8 9 10	1 2 3 4 5 6 7 8 9 10 11 12 13 14 15
		1 2 3 4 5	1 2 3 4 5 6 7 8 9 10	1 2 3 4 5 6 7 8 9 10 11 12 13 14 15
		1 2 3 4 5	1 2 3 4 5 6 7 8 9 10	1 2 3 4 5 6 7 8 9 10 11 12 13 14 15

Answer Keys

Starter 1—Gold
Build Comprehension

A 1. a
2. a
3. b
4. b
5. a

Learn about Words

B 1. grow
2. know
3. snow
4. row
5. crow

C 6. know
7. grow
8. Crow
9. snow
10. row

Focus on Skills

D 1. b
2. a
3. b
4. a
5. a

Starter 2—Gold
Build Comprehension

A 1. a
2. a
3. b
4. b
5. b

Learn about Words

B 1. mat
2. that
3. fat
4. sat
5. cat

C 6. sat
7. cat
8. that
9. fat
10. mat

Focus on Skills

D 1. No
2. Yes
3. No
4. Yes
5. No

Starter 3—Brown
Build Comprehension

A 1. b
2. b
3. a
4. a
5. a

Learn about Words

B 1. races
2. parks
3. miles
4. improvements
5. questions

C 6. parks
7. improvements
8. questions
9. races
10. miles

Focus on Skills

D 1. b
2. b
3. a
4. b
5. a

Starter 4—Lime
Build Comprehension

A 1. b
2. a
3. a
4. b
5. b

Learn about Words

B 1. scrambled
2. scolded
3. terms
4. produce
5. considered

C 6. scrambled
7. produce
8. considered
9. terms
10. scolded

Focus on Skills

D 1. b
2. a
3. a
4. a
5. b

E 6. walked
7. sold
8. what
9. friend
10. said

Starter 5—Olive
Build Comprehension

A 1. b
2. a
3. b
4. a
5. a

Learn about Words

B 1. blistering
2. proclaimed
3. inform
4. preparing
5. figured

C 6. inform
7. figured
8. blistering
9. proclaimed
10. preparing

Focus on Skills

D 1. hot
2. turtle
3. mouse
4. cool
5. white

E 6. girlfriend
7. swimsuit
8. sunglasses
9. houseboat
10. catfish

Starter 6—Blue
Build Comprehension

A 1. c
2. a
3. b
4. a
5. a

Learn about Words

B 1. announced
2. steadily
3. investigate
4. considered
5. submitted
6. present
7. achieve
8. accomplished

C 9. b
10. a

Focus on Skills

D 1. middle
2. middle
3. beginning
4. end
5. beginning

E 6. did not
7. could not
8. Do not
9. Here is
10. I will